Daydreams and Nightmares

Daydreams and Nightmares

Reflections on a Harlem Childhood

Irving Louis Horowitz

University Press of Mississippi
JACKSON AND LONDON

To Michael L. Lewin, *healer,* and Edward J. Bloustein,
builder

Library of Congress Cataloging-in-Publication Data

Horowitz, Irving Louis.
    Daydreams and nightmares : reflections on a Harlem childhood /
Irving Louis Horowitz.
        p.   cm.
    ISBN 0-87805-428-6 (alk. paper)
        1. Horowitz, Irving Louis—Childhood and Youth.   2. Jews—New York
(N.Y.)—Biography.   3. Harlem (New York, N.Y.)—Biography.   4. Afro-
Americans—New York (N.Y.)—Relations with Jews.   5. Social
scientists—United States—Biography.   6. New York (N.Y.)—
Biography.   I. Title.
    F128.9.J5H57   1990
    974.7'1004924—dc20   89-25054
                                                                    CIP

British Library Cataloguing-in-Publication data
available

CONTENTS

Even autobiographies are created in literary contexts, and this one is no exception. Above all, I was guided by H.L. Mencken's *A Choice of Days*. Mencken, with his gift for plain yet highly evocative language, was a master of uncompromising self-analysis, without a trace of self-flagellation or gratuitous self-praise. Another splendid guide was George Orwell. His prewar essays—in particular, "Down and Out" and "Wigan Pier"—are testimony that writing about childhood and youth need not be a celebration of innocence. François Truffaut caught something of this Orwellian spirit in the film *400 Blows*.

At first it seemed odd to me that two people as different as Mencken and Orwell could provide me with a common "model." Certainly, the politics of these two was not of primary importance. And just as assuredly, neither was their race, religion, or nationality. I was deeply impressed, though, by the literary ethic they shared—being able to write about the past as an unsentimental journey, and to do so with a keen sense of the severe discipline needed to live through it all; this combined with a parallel set of passions to understand the drama that is still being lived. Finally, both Mencken and Orwell liked words enormously. They were masters of language in general, and of English in particular. If my reflections fail to measure up to the standards set by my chosen literary guides, I at least have had the privilege of walking behind some mighty good companions.

The choice of models is one thing, the reason for writing about one's personal life is quite another. I had, in fact, long ago determined to resist any temptation to embark on such a project. For one, I felt that it would amount to a surrender of the future to the past; a looking backward rather than forward, and hence a rather rude if circumstantial admission that the best creative years of my life were behind me. For another, I felt that such work is, on the face of it, hubris—a surrender to the sin of pride. A well-written account of a person's life has nothing to do with that person's worth. To me, lives are led—the degree of importance measured by those who live them. Finally, the opportunity to falsify past realities is tempting. Fictional elements all too readily emerge, waiting to be slipped in almost without a conscious awareness. The question of veracity, then, reinforced my long-held resistance to begin an autobiography.

What finally tipped the scales against silence and for this limited effort was the more than twenty years I spent in researching a biography of the late C. Wright Mills, entitled *An American Utopian*. I discovered that much of what I knew about myself figured in the writing of this book. For example, in describing Mills's experiences at Columbia University I found myself reflecting on how the cliffs of Morningside Heights divided black and white, rich and poor, educated and illiterate when I was growing up. I saw Columbia from the distinct perspective of the Harlem "valley," not the Morningside "heights." To write intensely about another person is to think with equal intensity about one's self.

I also began to realize that the Millsian message, a crossover and intersection of the historical and the biographical, was at the core of the sociological imagination. The texture of the lives we lead serves as a subtle background for our social categorization. Thus, this re-creation of the first fourteen years of my life is an extension of my interest in describing a richer sociological mosaic. I called my biography of Mills a sociological biography—in contrast to an intellectual or intimate biography. I would like to think that the same is true in this effort at a fragmentary autobiography.

I should add that a practical impetus to this effort came about when I was asked in 1983 by my colleague Bennett Berger of the University of California at San Diego to contribute to a volume that he was assembling on the lives of well-known sociologists. I consented to participate in this project, but soon became entirely immersed in my formative childhood years. Although I had lost sight of the professional task at hand, Professor Berger and my friend James H. Clark of the University of California Press were nonetheless quite willing to include my contribution in their volume. I felt, however, that it had become too remote from the theme of "How I Became a Social Scientist" to merit inclusion. Anyhow, by the time I turned in that first draft to Bennett in 1985, the essay had already become too unwieldy to serve its initial purpose. And in the six years since that time, the manuscript has continued to evolve, by fits and starts, to its present size and scope. These things require a lengthy gestation period. One does not live a life in one sitting; nor should one write about a portion of a life in a swift and superficial way.

I suspect that the special nature of my childhood is such that this fragment of an autobiography will probably be all that there is. At least, at this point in my life, I believe this to be so. My later life is so much more conventional that a second autobiographical volume is hardly needed. Then, too, it is precisely the special nature of a Jewish childhood (well, that may be too strong; better say the childhood of a Jew) in Black Harlem that promises most to engage a reader. The departure from Harlem, and the end of childhood innocence and guilt alike, seems a reasonable cutoff point. I do add a chapter on the transition year from Harlem to Flatbush, since it took the larger part of that year to distance myself from my origins in order to mature and solidify.

Several friends, colleagues, and loved ones kindly offered good suggestions for improving my prose and checking the facts. I should like to thank Howard S. Becker, Bennett Berger, and Danielle Salti in particular for reading—and feeling—these thoughts on a childhood recaptured too late to be of much use to its author. My wife, Mary, who went through the Mills biography with me, also had the dubious distinction of going through this exercise. It was her constant probing and questioning that impelled me to answer hard questions about myself, no less than offer a narrative about other times and other people. Ralph Ellison, with whom it was my great, good fortune to share a classroom and a friendship at Bard in the late 1950s, and Isaac Bashevis Singer, whose precious writings link everything in God's world into a seamless whole of rationality and mystery, gave me confidence that the thin line of daydreams and nightmares can be traversed and communicated in a sensible way. The rest, as we said as kids, is just plain ancient history. To these people must be added the names of the two people connected with the nuts and bolts of publishing my effort: Richard M. Abel, director of the University Press of Mississippi, and Ann Mirels, whose copy-editing went beneath the skin of the manuscript into its soul.

Daydreams and Nightmares

It might instead be in fact, an instantaneous memory; we believe that what is happening to us has already happened before, as though the present time were splitting in two, breaking in its own midst into two parts: an immediate reality, plus a ghost of that reality.

Alain Robbe-Grillet, *Djinn*

In the Beginning

It has been said that Harlem is a state of mind. While this is so for any neighborhood, village, or turf, what distinguished Harlem, at least my Harlem, was its being a state within a state. More a casbah than a ghetto, it was a place with firm boundaries, as hard to get into as to get out of. Harlem was and remains a place of tenements, old apartments, brownstones. Harlem was and remains much more than a place of poverty. It is a way of life. From the Sugar Hill of the affluent to the Valley of the poor at the base of Morningside Heights, Harlem is a place of joys as well as a place of blues. I know this is true since Harlem remains part of my emotional texture no less than my geographical context.

The old *WPA Guide to New York City,* prepared by the Federal Writers' Project Guide in the late 1930s, caught this casbahlike spirit.

Negro Harlem, into which are crowded more than a quarter of a million Negroes from southern states, the West Indies, and Africa, has many different aspects. To whites seeking amusement, it is an exuberant, original, and unconventional entertainment center; to Negro college graduates it is an opportunity to practice a profession among their own people; to those aspiring to racial leadership it is a domain where they may advocate their theories unmolested; to artists, writers, and sociologists it is a mine of Black America.

And to those rare stray cats from the Ukrainian pale like the Horowitz family, it was a place to make a living and a place to grow up. To live there was to be a vilified Jewish minority within a mortified black minority, to use the imagery employed by Booker T. Washington in *The Man Farthest Down*.

Turf wars were bitter in Harlem because the area proved to be so inelastic. Unlike the usual neighborhoods of New York, there was little spillover and scarcely any movement at the boundaries. To the east, from Third Avenue to the East River-Triboro Bridge area, were the Italians; to the west, from Broadway to the Hudson River, were the Irish; to the south, below 110th Street, were the Puerto Rican immigrants; and to the north, around the cavernous divide of the Polo Grounds area, was Washington Heights, which in the 1930s contained a strongly Jewish enclave. Harlem, the capital of the black world, did not so much overlook a national entity as it was surrounded by seemingly alien forces.

What added emotional fuel to the economic fires of a depression-plagued area was a shared impoverishment. Every form of employment translated to an economic struggle of zero-sum game proportions. "You've got a job and I haven't" was the bottom line. No one spoke of enough to go around for all, or of expanding potentials for all participants. Harlem was a world of "have nots" whose rhetoric was wrapped up in the reverse: "You have, and I have not." The rationale for such intense social combat was the notion of an economic fixed pie. For every winner, there had to be a loser.

For special families who lived in the heart of Harlem, and not at its ecological or geographical edge, the situation was more complex. For those few Jewish merchants, shopkeepers, and even intellectuals who made Harlem their home, the turf wars and economic competition were in part, at least, overridden by a shared fate and common culture, and a sense of being inside rather than outside the capital of black America. That certainly was the case for my family.

The experience of Harlem convinced me that the relationship of blacks and Jews in America has special historical significance. This is not to make fatuous claims about harmony and common cause; rather, to assert that these two distinctly different peoples—sometimes marching arm in arm as in the civil rights struggle, other times in bitter confrontation as in Bedford-Stuyvesant—tell us much about the moral status of this nation at any given moment in time. They tell a story of aspirations realized and thwarted, cultures transmitted yet bowdlerized, and groups seeking security in race or religious solidarity up against individuals seeking to escape the boundaries of group life as such.

Unbeknownst to Harlemites, the relations of blacks and Jews were also a story of "models" and "antimodels"—what to do and what not to do in order to survive. Blacks seemed largely indifferent to Jewish ritual and tradition; nonetheless, they were strongly attracted to the Jewish ethic of family solidarity and social concern. There was an unpleasant side to this—a belief that even Jews without money had money. And there was an underlying concern that such money was a greater source of power than physical prowess. For their part, Jews viewed black physicality with more fear than respect. They also saw black argot, humor, and frank sexuality as a danger and risk. Yet, I was not alone in seeking to emulate what seemed to be a wild individualism coupled with a cultural life that marked the black Harlemites as freer in their ghetto than almost anyone else living in the larger environs of New York. Perhaps it is this sense of being free that distinguishes the ghetto from the casbah. Lord knows that it made the normative idea of personal reserve and divine guilt difficult to accept.

If the rest of pre-War America appeared unconcerned or insensitive to black societal problems or cultural achievements, this was not the case with the Jews. Even in the supreme black achievement of jazz, when Ellington, Basie, Webb, Lunceford, and the great black bands that played the Apollo in the late 1930s held sway, Jewish musicians—Goodman, Gershwin, Mezzrow, and Whiteman, among others—not only played the music, but also served as critics and interpreters. In a racially controlled pre-War America, it was the Jew who popularized black life, transforming a folk tradition into an art mode.

Although the close proximity of blacks and Jews in Harlem allowed for a rich cross-fertilization of cultures, it also engendered feelings of rivalry and resentment. Those who have nothing often see those who have little in sharpest relief. And in Harlem, the large mass of black people who had nothing were confronted by a small, fragmented subset of Jews who had at least a little something—small shops, property, and seemingly secure jobs. Above all, the Jews seemed to be able to move in and out of Harlem with an ease denied all but a handful of black ghetto-dwellers.

Such unique interactions were scarcely greeted with loud shouts of joy on either side of the ghetto enclave. The blacks often saw their uniqueness compromised. Worse, it seemed that the gain and fame of their culture went to the accursed Jewish cultural middleman, while the purity of their performance remained undersupported and undernourished. The majority of Jews, for their part, saw this flirtation with black culture as nothing short of a desecration of Jewish life—an early warning signal that sexuality would displace marriage and undiluted individual expression would destroy family solidarity. While the music of a Thomas "Fats" Waller or the paintings of a Jacob Lawrence were imitated by a few Jews—the early advocates of the "white hipster" phenomenon—for most Jews, such expression was perceived as soul-destroying. But if Jolson's *Jazz Singer* offered only a parody of this condition, it was at least an acknowledgement of a larger life with which many Jews found themselves to be in secret sympathy—even as they publicly stated their abhorrence for such a strange culture.

Harlem in the 1930s was, among other things, a place where blacks and Jews met, exchanged ideas and sentiments, and even shared in the radical shibboleths of communism and socialism. But it was not a pure blend, or one that led to a new and higher unity. For blacks, by the end of the "proletarian" decade, the abstractions of socialism were replaced with the specificities of African nationalism; while for Jews, this same faith in socialism was dissolved by the even more specific economic results of Americanism at home coupled with the betrayal of democratic ideals at the diplomatic conference tables of Europe. About the only thing one could say with certainty about this period and place was that it had no parallel in the rest of American society.

For the most part, blacks remained "invisible" to most Americans; or if visible, then only by virtue of "knowing their place" in the complex social and economic hierarchy that evolved mainly in the South, and then elsewhere in America as the black migration spread to the North and to the West. The Jews of Harlem, if my extended family was any barometer, were viewed as dregs—social scourges and economic failures—simply by virtue of the fact that they remained.

By the decade of the thirties, the Jews of Harlem were few in number, visible in their occupations and unusual in their insistence on residing in a black stronghold while their brethren fled to greener parts of New York City. Even if they worked in central Harlem, Jews often lived on the edges, the peripheries of Harlem, where their synagogues and social institutions were located. They were a vilified culture, fearfully sharing the capital of the black race. Ellis Island was a processing plant, but Harlem was the settlement village for Jews completely without money.

The center of joys and sorrows in Harlem—the dorsal spine—was 125th Street. There one found the Hotel Theresa, the Apollo Theater, the Loews and Alhambra-RKO, and the Harlem Community Art Center. The main shopping district of Harlem, 125th Street radiated out, and we, the children of 123rd Street, gravitated toward the center. We never walked through the side streets of Harlem. We ran. Only along the main thoroughfares (125th, 135th, 145th, and 155th) did we dare pause to walk. Not to run was to fight, perhaps risk being killed. Being fleet-footed helped. So did knowing every sanctuary and landmark that were part of the landscape of the ghetto. To write about a Harlem childhood, the private imagination in search of a romantic past must be cast aside. Sensibility was trapped in sociability; imagination was caught on the fly, on the sly, and on the run.

What follows is in large measure a series of episodes rather than a systematic narrative. As Piaget long ago discovered, the logic of children is largely staccato—a series of rests between successive acts. This experiential vision stands the autobiographer in good stead, since the human mind tends to recall things in terms of extremes. And these peaks and caverns of experience form the backbone of my early recollections.

The title *Daydreams and Nightmares* stems from the fact that my private thoughts often paralleled a public life of great aspirations and even greater tragedies. Every day was a risk. Others have told me that as children they never feared for their lives—they never felt threatened by hostile forces. This seems strange to me, since in my Harlem upbringing, issues of life and death presented themselves to me routinely. Indeed, I determined early that to ignore the possibility that the thin thread of life could be snuffed out was to invite that prospect to become more feasible. In that profound sense, not only was my upbringing very remote from that of other white Jewish children of the middle classes, but as I have since come to learn, very close to that of black Christian children of the underclasses with whom I shared a common turf and apparently an uncommonly keen sense of the finitude of existence. The stuff of daydreams and nightmares is made up precisely of issues related to life and death.

CHAPTER ONE

Through metaphorical concentration, doctors can imagine
what it is to be their patients. Those who have no pain can
imagine those who suffer. Those at the center can imagine
what it is to be outside. The strong can imagine the weak.
Illuminated lives can imagine the dark. Poets in their
twilight can imagine the borders of stellar fire. We
strangers can imagine the familiar hearts of strangers.
    Cynthia Ozick, *Metaphor & Memory*

The Metropolitan
and Sydenham

To start with, the process of Americanization began at birth.
Within the space of one week at the Metropolitan Hospital, I
started life as a Hebrew child, with the name Yitzhak-Isaac. This
apparently was too cumbersome for record-keeping purposes, so
I was entered on the birth certificate as Isadore. But my sister, or at
least so she told me, thought that name far too Europeanized for a
Harlem baby, so I became Irving by the seventh day. Louis is an
affectation of my late teens—there had to be a way to distinguish
myself from all the other Irvings who lived in the Bronx and
Brooklyn. One would hope that at least some of them have less
pedestrian explanations of the birth and transfiguration of identity.

For most people the Met is an opera house; for me it was a place
to be born. The Metropolitan Hospital on the northern end of
Welfare Island represented a bridge between Manhattan and

Queens. For some reason it was always thought of as an extension of Manhattan, probably because it was tied to Tammany Hall politics throughout the first part of the century. The shuttle and the ferry to the Metropolitan from Manhattan were available at 78th Street. Turf is a scarce commodity in New York City. People fight for every square inch of it. In that sense, too, the Metropolitan Hospital was very much part of Manhattan. It was one of the largest welfare hospitals in the city, equipped to give free services to the city's poor. Ironically, for many years it also housed a prison. No one in those days thought of anyone in Queens as being poor, although to be at the Metropolitan was to be poor.

My mother told me that she had an omen about me (she never did specify whether it was a good or evil omen). In fact, I was born deformed, and worse, came out without a breath. She had to make a decision: keep her baby alive, or let it sink into a coma and write off the whole nine-month experience as a bad dream. This was hardly an era that recognized intensive neonatal care. And from my mother's account, the loss of one more poor child would not exactly have been greeted with sobs in the nursing quarters.

My mother's choice to keep me alive meant breathing life into me via mouth-to-mouth resuscitation. She worked at this for several long hours, but when color came to my face and the inevitable big cry emanated from me, the deed had been done. I had been chosen for life. So there I was, at the northern tip of aptly named Welfare Island—an occupant of one of 1,385 beds—or so I am told by the *WPA Guide to New York City*. This was but the start of my working familiarity with the hospitals of New York. Once born, the problem was to survive.

The other hospital that was a pivot of my childhood days was "Syd," or Sydenham, located at Hancock Place at the western-most point of 125th Street. The name derived from the great seventeenth-century English physician and close friend of John Locke, Thomas Sydenham. The hospital was a stately but intimate five-story structure built early in the century, no doubt to service a stately clientele. Placards listed the names of donors of a bygone era, of British and Dutch Protestant wealth, along with the more recent German-Jewish staff. "Syd" was situated only a few blocks from my parents' shop; getting to it was even easier for me than getting to school.

Reminiscence automatically conjures present-day meanings. In the case of the Metropolitan and Sydenham it was a veritable ransoming of the past. The daily demonstrations in front of Sydenham several years ago was for most people simply another manifestation of the ongoing struggle between local and city control, between the rigors of an economy and the necessities of a community; poignant, yes, but by this time rather tame stuff— except for those of us who had to live through the experience of the Met and Sydenham. One thinks of *people* as dying, not hospitals. Hospitals endure—eternal, mystical representations of the frailties and limits of human endurance—the seamier side of church life. I should add that my knowledge of the Met is somewhat limited because by the time I was five all my records had been transferred from there to Sydenham. My mother insisted that I was stillborn and that she breathed life into me after doctors at the Met had given up. Whether this is apocryphal or hyperbolic is almost beside the point. She remembered it that way, and transmitted to me the trauma of birth.

The doctors at the Met between 1929 and 1935 were, I presume, New York's finest. I vaguely remember them as competent, but in a child's mind doctors represent more than competence; they represent assurance of survival by special people uniquely interested in life. Of my first five years on earth, roughly two and one-half were spent at the Met and something like ten operations were performed on me starting with several soon after birth. My mother said that I never came home until I reached the age of one. This is not the kind of subject I was likely to contest, or of which she was likely to be unsure. After all, every day in the hospital meant one less mouth to feed. And what a mouth!

Cleft palate and harelip victims were and remain a special problem for plastic reconstruction, or as it's more commonly known, plastic surgery. The techniques prevalent at the time of my birth were still relatively primitive—although not primitive in the same sense as fifty years earlier, when harelips and cleft palates were simply sent to madhouses or asylums of one kind or another, given up as lost causes. The basic technique was stitching the soft front palate to the palate roof. It was a serviceable operation, but not performed with the aesthetic or cosmetic criteria people have now come to expect from plastic surgery. The reason for the large number of operations was that bleeding was profuse, and stitches could be removed only after sufficient healing time. This was followed by another round of surgery. Each surgical procedure was discrete; no thought was given to combining or clustering them. And scarcely any attention was paid to how the patient looked, much less felt.

I recently had occasion to visit Montefiore Hospital, where no fewer than a team of seven people minister to the child in need of surgery, including a trained child psychologist. The luxury of a team of seven stunned me. I only then realized what a dynamic field plastic surgery had become. Stitching people now seems to signify some type of medical failure; even the hint of a scar is viewed as a botch.

This is not to complain. I was privy to several historical accidents that gave me the best medical attention available anywhere in the world. I was the "beneficiary" of fascism; famous doctors and surgeons from Berlin and Vienna were pouring out of Europe during my adolescence. The pioneers of advanced techniques of plastic surgery often found themselves immigrants on the same Ellis Island through which my parents had passed only a decade or two earlier. Harlem had a desperate, crying need for medical practitioners. Doctors from European exile often ended up interning at Harlem hospitals. The most famous names in European surgery were treating the poorest families in Harlem. Indeed, my first contact with European intellectual life was through its extraordinary surgeons—a breed of Jews further removed culturally from my family than we were from our black neighbors in Harlem.

It was not until I reached adulthood that I understood the technical problems involved in massive facial reconstruction. Every procedure involved a great deal of cutting, bone-breaking and resetting, and stitching—all in some way combined with a sense of aesthetics; that is, how the face as a whole would look after a particular procedure was accomplished and the swelling reduced. In the mind of the child, or in my mind at least, the goal was hard to perceive, whereas the means—the blows—were all too real. Thus, with every new operation I improved my appearance, my speech, my facial structure; but at the same time, I became increasingly demoralized—overwhelmed by the thought that this search for a perfect face would never end. Well, perhaps the notion of perfection overstates the case; it was more a search for a minimally adequate appearance after so much torment, suffering, hospitalization.

The reason for my visit to Montefiore was to see my old doctor, Michael Lewin, now chief of plastic reconstruction, and even in the mid-1930s highly regarded. The occasion was the death of his uncle, Dr. Edward Maliniac. It is almost axiomatic that a child confronted with the name Maliniac would reduce it to "maniac" in an instant. For me, he became forever "Dr. Maniac." I might add he got his revenge on me by handling me very roughly indeed. I knew it was rough because I never had the same pain after being treated by Dr. Lewin. But in truth, there was never any doubt in my mind that Dr. Maliniac and Dr. Lewin were my saviors. Their caring and concern made up for a great deal. It gave me hope and helped me carry on.

The routine was generally the same. After all my records had been shifted to Sydenham, I would visit the offices of Maliniac and Lewin (which as I recollect were in a posh Park Avenue portion of downtown Manhattan), followed by a trip to the medical photographer located in the old Paramount Building in midtown Manhattan. He had contraptions and mechanisms for expanding the size of a child's mouth the likes of which have not been seen since medieval torture chambers. The photos would then be picked up and delivered to the offices of the good doctors who would then determine the next surgical procedure. This in turn was followed by a visit to the inevitable social welfare division of Sydenham to arrange for the usual free bed and free hospital care. The doctors never bothered billing my parents; they simply billed their wealthy clientele twice or three times the regular billing. By magic everything seemed to work fine in this homespun version of socialist reallocation of wealth.

While the doctors were extraordinarily selfless and worked without any direct recompense—certainly none from either the hospital or my parents—they did make use of me as a test case. Every procedure, painfully limited, was written up in a variety of plastic surgery journals. By the age of nine or ten my loud mouth had invaded many scholarly medical journals; always with the before and after pictures, always with the same presumption of success, and always with the heartrending conclusion of more surgical work to come. The work of medical science never ends!

Between the ages of five and thirteen I was a regular inhabitant of Sydenham—a pillar of hospital patient society. I spent at least four to five months annually in that hospital, always following the same routine: entrance, examination, surgery, recovery period, and healing period. Then, another surgery cycle initiated after a semester at school.

I had as a child, and still retain, a dread fear of ether or any masks over or near my face. Anything that puts me to sleep unwillingly—laughing gas, nerve gas, ether—even the chemical smells, sights, and sounds of a hospital—all fuse and merge into an overwhelming feeling of hopeless rebellion and rage. I often think that I was spared any drug habit in Harlem, or in adult life, because every thought of needles, syringes, or paraphernalia raised the spectre of hospital life.

But this limitation on anaesthesia also meant that the surgical procedures were extremely vivid and painful. Three- to five-hour operations seemed like an eternity. And the two most dreaded ordeals were the hammer banging incessantly away at my nose and facial bone structure and the process of stitching. The "locals" did indeed kill almost all the pain. But it turns out that there are two sorts of pain: real and symbolic. Even as the surgeon is assuring you that "you won't feel a thing," the human mind envisions the procedure precisely—and the imagined pain is no less agonizing than the real.

In the world of primitive anesthesiology, survival went to those best equipped to endure the pain—the pain of anticipating the surgery; the pain of the surgery itself; and the pain connected with weeks (sometimes months) of postoperative recovery. If courage means coping with the actual and cowardice fearing the unknown, then I was fortunate in having much of the former and being spared the latter. In some strange way, this served me well later in life. In the world of sports, in basketball in particular, where the surrender of the body to the goal of a score is so central, the pain connected with the event seemed modest compared with the intensity of the pain of surgery. Still, I wouldn't recommend surgery as a means for instilling the sportive instinct.

In those days, my being in the hospital was a kind of liberation for my parents. It meant one less mouth to feed for four to six months a year. This was no small consideration for a family of four living on fifty cents a day. My hospitalization freed my mother to work alongside my father, or better liberated him to go on his rounds and repair one more lock, replace one more molding, or build one more frame. Under such circumstances, the hospital became a total institution for me—a sort of benign prison with daily or weekly visitations from my parents and the doctors and nurses. Then there were my own visits to every other ward and every other division of Sydenham. I knew every floor, every room, and every service performed by doctors, nurses, and orderlies. I would wander about to all parts of the hospital despite the constant warnings that I was not to leave the floor. The one floor they didn't have to warn me about was the fifth, where surgery was performed. Those heavy bright lights with the green tint seemed constantly to shine—they shined through all my dreams, all my nightmares. I would never voluntarily take the elevator that went to the surgical floor. Curiosity had its limits.

The hospital was a world unto itself. It was the "school" at which I became an autodidact. At that time, children who were long-term patients had to teach themselves, since there were no formal education programs. This proved a blessing in disguise; it removed me from the everyday terrors of public schooling in Harlem—teachers who were shredding me, kids who were chasing me, and others who were content to ridicule me. The hospital was a retreat, a monastery more than a prison. In its environs nobody was laughable—everything strange was normal.

The most important event was the book-cart rounds. The cart brought new reading matter each day: everything from V.I. Lenin's *What is to be done?* to Defoe's *Robinson Crusoe*. I don't remember ever reading a book at Sydenham specifically intended for children; there was a *Tom Swift* series, but these books were read by everyone. There were also comic books; and at the tender age of nine it did not strike me as unusual to go from Batman to

Superman to Leninman. In retrospect, I think Sydenham was where I picked up the habit of reading anything and everything without regard to genre or format.

Of course there were no television sets; the medium had barely been invented. Radios were not allowed in the children's wing, for reasons not explained. Thus, reading became a primary activity for everyone. These were no fancy private rooms; Sydenham will never be confused with the Waldorf-Astoria. All children lived in wards, not rooms. There were eight to sixteen children to a ward. The only time we had a private room was on the day prior to surgery and following surgery, in the recovery room. There were so many children coming and going, so many short-term patients, that it was hard to establish friendships. Through my own suffering I developed a keen appreciation for the suffering of others. There was a feeling of shared battle, which was constantly reinforced by doctors, parents, and other patients as well: "Irving you think you have problems; take a look around you." And, indeed, when I did look around, I saw other children with maladies far worse than my own.

There were few deaths reported in the children's wing—much suffering and much pain, but not much dying. Somehow, though, everyone knew when someone had died in another ward or in another room. An eerie pall would settle over an uneasy quiet; nurses and orderlies murmuring. We knew that someone else had passed away. Those were always bad days, sometimes only bad hours; feelings and emotions change rapidly in hospitals. On the day of departure from the hospital, feelings were most intense: the morning of dressing and the goodbyes and tears of those left behind. The worst days were surgery days, with the needles, drugs, preparations—a host of doctors and nurses busying themselves over your poor carcass. I became depersonalized, and no matter how many times (it must have been fourteen at Sydenham and ten at the Metropolitan) I went under the knife, it was always a confrontation of the ultimate sort, a vague disbelief in the possibility of recovery, a bitterness that the external world was at work and play while I was estranged in a hospital. Tears were mixed with anxiety. I was fortunate with my doctors who knew in a very profound way what each child endured. The doctors' visits were what we lived for—the proof that we were alive, and that someone cared.

The surgery cycle kept me both alive and marginal to the world of the Harlem streets. The Met and Sydenham broke the cycle of wildness, petty theft, gang war, and street aggression. It interrupted the ordinary flow of life, and in doing so probably saved my life. Of all the people I recollect from those days, I'm the only survivor from 123rd Street and 8th Avenue. The streets brought an early death to many of the healthy, the strong, and the courageous of my peers. My infirmity strangely protected me. If during moments of great suffering, I couldn't see things with quite such dialectical finesse, I at least understood that while I was being denied some of life's best chances, I was also being spared much of the worst.

My mixed blessings came to an end very close upon the achievement of manhood, at the age of thirteen. I went to the offices of Dr. Lewin where we went through the familiar routine: postsurgery review, postsurgery photographs, and the inevitable call for a next round of operations. The work of a good plastic surgeon, not unlike that of a good sculptor, is never finished. The deformed human body becomes the putty on which to create perfection. The difficulty is that the human body is not an inanimate object, but a thinking, feeling being.

On this particular occasion, Dr. Lewin, my personal Michaelangelo, explained to me that the next procedure was called the push-back, in which the tissue of the soft palate would be brought from the rear and connected to the hard palate so as to reduce the nasality of my voice and further close up a lingering gap in the roof of my mouth. This "black hole" not only prevented food from being digested, but caused some to reflux and be expelled through my nostrils. This was none too pleasant, either for me to endure or for others to watch. My parents readily agreed to the next operation, but this time the patient was unwilling.

A decision, my decision, had to be made between medical improvement and personal capacity to endure more of the torture of hospitals and surgical procedures. My nerves were simply worn too thin. I had become too frightened, too antagonistic to the whole cycle of hospitalization and surgery. The question for me was whether I could survive without another operation, and what could be done short of surgery to improve matters. The push-back operation never took place. Years later, an alternative nonsurgical dental procedure closed my upper palate. On that day, at the age of thirteen, I determined that however I looked at that point was how I was going to look, and that however I spoke at that point was how I was going to speak. On that day in my doctor's office, rather than in front of an indifferent congregation at synagogue, I became a man: I made a critical decision for myself and by myself.

CHAPTER TWO

The promised land was a slum ghetto. There was a
tremendous difference in the way life was lived up North.
There were too many people filled with hate and bitterness
crowded into a dirty, stinky, uncared-for closet-size section
of a great city. . . . The children of these disillusioned
colored pioneers inherited the total lot of their parents the
disappointments, the anger. To add to their misery, they
had little hope of deliverance. For where does one run to
when he's already in the promised land?

Claude Brown, *Manchild in the Promised Land*

Black Christmas

Sydenham Hospital was not just a place I went to for surgery. It
was the hub of social work and social welfare for central Harlem
in the mid-1930s. It was a world of goods and services. Anything I
needed or wanted—anything that could not be provided at
home—initiated a trip to Sydenham. The second floor had a
section designated "Social Welfare," the most frequented part of
the hospital by the poor and the infirm. And that included just
about everyone.

It was Social Welfare that permitted patients to have surgery
without charge, or at bare minimum cost. It was often supervised
by nursing personnel rather than professional social-work agents.
There was a good sense for what patients needed, even if advice
tended to be routine. This section of the hospital was also in
charge of summer fresh-air funds that enabled the children of the
poor to escape from the ghetto areas for a two-week vacation. The
aura of the hospital helped overcome the resistance of families,

especially of Jewish families for whom self-reliance was a mark of survival, to the very idea of welfare. Calling such assistance "social" rather than "economic" also helped. Welfare became linked to the concept of human amenities rather than bare-boned economic assistance.

My most vivid recollection of this outpatient function centered on Christmas, 1938. I had discovered the joys—the religion—of baseball. The New York Giants were Manhattan's team. Winning the pennant in 1936 and 1937 didn't hurt. I asked my mother stompingly and tearfully for a baseball, bat, and glove. I was immediately informed that first of all these things were not an entitlement; second, there was no money for such purchases; and third, they were sinful. The sin was not in baseball artifacts as such, but in demanding *Christmas* gifts. Jewish children it appeared didn't receive Christmas gifts. Therein lay the sin—first in asking for the gifts, and second, in thinking such artifacts were worth possessing.

In this instance, tears persisted and prevailed. Having discovered the New York Giants lived and worked at 155th Street, and having adopted them as my personal team and totem, the next step was owning a bat, ball, and glove—no matter what the cost or penalty. Only by this means could I one day become a member of the great Giant organization—the dream of every boy born under the shadow of Coogan's Bluff.

As did every hospital, Sydenham had an outpatient Christmas celebration after which Santa Claus gave out the gifts that had been signed up for weeks earlier. There was never any question as to what I would receive once the deal had been struck between the social services department and my mother. The trick was simply showing up and getting home with the gifts; no mean trick as it turned out. The great expected day arrived—December 24th. There was a long corridor in the children's wing (I knew it well since at least ten of my twenty-four operations had been conducted there) where the Christmas party was to commence.

If, for my parents, the whole business of Christmas and Santa Claus bordered on the sacrilegious, for me it became something bordering on metaphysics—and the abstract can be frightening. I knew all about Santa Claus, having seen him in every newspaper and magazine; but I had never seen a black Santa Claus. Two hundred black children, poor as I was or poorer, three nurses whose race I can't recollect, and a fearsome-looking black Santa Claus. Urine ran hot in my pants before my name was called. I knew it would be my turn with the melodic bowdlerization: "Hawitz." I had begun to identify my name as Hawitz, pronounced with the southern inflection of the blacks who frequented my father's shop.

The wait seemed interminable. More than a few eyes glared at me. I had no doubt that the other children thought of me as an interloper, whose very presence served to reduce the value, or at least the quantity, of their own goods. One whispered in my ear, "Boy, you may get those presents but you ain't never goin' to use 'em." Such asides didn't add to my feeling of security. Finally, my name was called. I dutifully stepped forward and sat on Black Santa's lap. He asked me what I wanted for Christmas—a rhetorical question, of course, since my packet contained exactly what Social Welfare had told my mother that I would receive. Without any sense of being overjoyed, I accepted the gifts. The next step, the hard step, was getting home with the booty.

My normal pattern in those days was to be given a schedule different from the other children. The arrangement with the principal of P.S. 125 stipulated my leaving earlier. But there was no such arrangement with Sydenham Hospital. Hence, I duly waited with my gifts in hand until everyone's name had been called. Then, with a heavy heart, I left the hospital compound after all the others had gone. Outside, I confronted the heavy wooden side gates of Sydenham, which I had always greeted with foreboding, as if entering would shut out the entirety of the real world permanently and absolutely. On this occasion I would have relished a respite from the real world, for outside those gates were my inevitable tormentors: other neighborhood welfare children. One came up to me saying very matter-of-factly, "Fuckface, you can gimme the ball, the bat, and the glove or we can take 'em from you. You can run home and not get hurt or you can stay here and get hard-punished." Almost as if we had been conducting a business transaction, I turned over the ball, the bat, and the glove in silence. I was allowed to walk away, near tears, with a despair grounded in the shame of not having fought, but mixed with relief at being alive. When I got back home—or better to the store, as it was—my mother asked me where all the *goyish* presents were. I soberly explained what had happened, whereupon she replied without pity, "I told you Christmas isn't a Jewish holiday." This may have taught me a lesson about Christianity, but it hardly endeared me to Judaism.

All wrongs are eventually righted, or a better way of putting matters, all rights are wronged. Christmas wasn't only a time of personal pain; it was also a special occasion on which my father wreaked his own revenge on Christendom. The week before Christmas nearly every black family brought in electric light bulbs—Christmas ornaments—to be tested. These bulbs, imported from Japan (and in those days that meant cheap, not good), retailed for ten cents each. The colored bulbs were used only on rare occasions—the week before Christmas and perhaps the week during Christmas. They burned out quickly; but not that quickly. My father developed a testing technique for examining these bulbs which always proved more costly to the customer than it should have.

The scam went like this: The unsuspecting customer would bring in all light bulbs for testing. Each bulb would be placed against the side of the bulb tester rather than against the filament that would light up the bulb. The trick was easily learned and passed on to my mother, my sister, and me. I became a master at this special bulb test. When the same bulbs were retested after the customer left, they almost always were found to be perfect, or at least good enough for resale. My father placed them into inventory and sold them as new. The special bulbs were resold countless times each season. Hence, it was no accident that the volume of December bulb sales probably surpassed that of any other month. December profits also showed remarkably uncharacteristic good health. 'Twas, indeed, the season to be merry.

I don't know how many improperly tested bulbs made up for how many stolen bats, balls, and gloves. But somewhere the good Lord in His infinite wisdom apportioned criminality among his impoverished children so perfectly that no one was likely to end up the winner or the loser. The Christmas period enabled everyone to set aside, at least for one day, the little murders of the heart that took place the rest of the year—especially the week before the arrival of the baby Jesus.

CHAPTER THREE

Daily and nightly the pageant of Harlem takes place on
125th Street, a spectacle spontaneously staged by
Harlemites for Harlemites. The commotion is unbelieva-
ble. Everything, even casual window shopping, is
conducted in a kind of frenzy . . . The sound on the stage
of the Apollo is just a refinement of the noise outside—
infinitely more disciplined of course, but still echoing its
environment.
  Jack Schiffman, *Uptown: The Story of Harlem's Apollo
  Theatre*

To a Wild Rose

Some years ago the great tenor saxophonist Sonny Rollins record-
ed "To a Wild Rose" by Edward MacDowell. Either Mr. Rollins
went to the same public school—P.S. 125—that I did, or one with
a similar exotic classical music curriculum. One of the great
anomalies of growing up absurd at P.S. 125 was the musical offer-
ings. Here we sat at 123rd Street and Hancock Place, thirty-five
black students and two whites, singing (or at least feigning to
sing) "serious" music.

In the educational environment of the Great Depression, there
was a heavy cultural emphasis on the American melting pot. Every
course of music was divided between European classical and
American classical—or what passed as American classical, since
neither George Gershwin nor Benny Goodman figured in the
panoply of greats. Enter Edward MacDowell and "To a Wild
Rose." It was played by a scratchy ensemble on a scratchy 78-rpm
record. We all had to learn "To a Wild Rose," and we all were

notified that it was an American classic. But to us, or at least to me, the music was irritating. Its melodic tranquility seemed at odds with the environment, even emotionally absurd.

We learned other brief ditties. In a sing-song fashion we were taught that the Eighth Symphony was "the symphony that Schubert wrote and never finished." And we dutifully learned about "Papa" Haydn and his more than one hundred symphonies. But not a word about "Fatha" Earl Hines and his more than one hundred jazz piano recordings. No wonder we were confused about Western culture—what it was, where it began, how it evolved. Jazz was part of the life of Harlem. Big words like culture and civilization remained in school.

These were also the times between 1937 and 1940 when at least once a week my sister Paula took me to the Apollo. We saw everyone from Count Basie to Duke Ellington to Billy Eckstine to Lionel Hampton. The atmosphere of Harlem, if nothing else, was entirely musical. Everyone danced, children and old people. The music of the day was big-band swing or some variation of ensemble jazz. Every big band came to the Apollo; the very act of being invited was somehow a "laying on of hands." Charlie Barnet might have made five times as much at the Paramount downtown, and he probably did, but I'm sure that the "White Duke," as he came to be called at the Apollo, was an appellation that neither he nor his band would part with easily. Playing the Apollo Opera House meant a bond between audience and orchestra that permitted musical freedom. It was a statement of quality.

There were probably few in a typical Apollo audience who listened to Haydn, Schubert, or MacDowell. Most hadn't even heard of them. Yet, these people were ardent fans of music and were sophisticated consumers. The Apollo audience sat in unwavering collective judgment of the good, the bad, and the mediocre. From billboards posted throughout Harlem, everyone knew who was performing and when. These billboards seemed to be manufactured by the same marketing mavens who posted notices for the prizefights at Madison Square Garden. Major figures' names were in giant type, lesser names in type not so large, and newcomers' names were printed small. The billboards lent Harlem a sense of community, of intimacy. And it made the Apollo an even more special place than one simply of top-flight entertainment. The Apollo united audience and performer in a way that I have never seen duplicated—save for festivals in New Orleans.

Stories abound about amateur night at the Apollo with the habitues of the second balcony putting out the hooks and dragging some would-be Ella Fitzgerald offstage howling and screaming. The fact is that every night was amateur night at the Apollo. The Apollo audience took its music with absolute seriousness, demanding a professional refinement inside the theater of the sights and sounds heard on the streets. Comparisons between Chick Webb and Count Basie were real. That so many bandleaders had titles of nobility attached to their names is indicative of the esteem in which they were held. If a black man couldn't be president, he could at least be a duke, an earl, or a count. In Harlem, the Apollo was a universal musical mecca. No one was kept out on the basis of age, sex, color, or creed. My sister and I were there every week, or as frequently as there was a change of program.

In those days the live performance was punctuated by ancient films, usually as dreadful as the owners—Frank, Jack, and Bob Schiffman—could find. Had it been otherwise, they never would have been able to get anybody out of their seats to let in newcomers for the next performance. Even so, with an hour and a half of live performance and three hours of dead film, the movement in the audience was remarkably slow. Sitting through three performances, or twelve hours, was not uncommon for the regulars. I ought to know, being one of them. And after it was all over, confronting the night air always proved something of a shock.

In a place from which Harlem's showcase to the world was one block removed, listening to Edward MacDowell every single week until I learned to sing "To a Wild Rose" properly was a painful experience. Through no fault of his own, I grew up hating poor MacDowell; it took me many years to come to listen to "Papa" Haydn, even though I liked him but did not know who he was; and Schubert's "Unfinished" Symphony remains about the only work he wrote that has no compelling power for me.

Imagine, then, how terrific it was to listen years later to Sonny Rollins's rendition of "To a Wild Rose" and sense that somewhere, way back then, he too was in a room—perhaps similar to my own—sharing the same bifurcated cultural experience: listening to a world of alien music being defined as American, while jazz for its part was defined as alien and culturally deformed.

The miracle of it all, though, was not the loathing of Mac-Dowell, but the gradual identification of avant-garde black music with twentieth-century classicism. With the coming of the 1940s—with Minton's Playhouse on 119th Street and Small's Paradise on Seventh Avenue; with the beginnings of the "modern" sounds of Lester Young, Dizzy Gillespie, and Charlie Parker—similarities to Bartok, Stravinsky, Piston, and Prokofiev became evident. For me listening to "serious" music meant starting with the present and working my way backward. My first "classical" listening experience was Stravinsky's *Firebird Suite;* then I graduated to the six Bartok quartets. My friend Harvey Cropper heard through the grapevine that the giants of European composition had the swinging sense. And I'm now happy to report that I've finally come to enjoy Edward MacDowell—thanks in large part to "late" Sonny Rollins and P.S. 125.

CHAPTER FOUR

Central Park is of great importance as the first real park
made in this country—a democratic development of the
highest significance and on the success of which, in my
opinion, much of the progress of art and aesthetic culture
in this country is dependent.
     Frederick Law Olmstead, *Forty Years of Landscape
Architecture*

Central Park

Central Park in the 1930s was truly a people's park. Not by any
municipal proclamation, but simply because everyone went there.
It was the nightly retreat for Manhattanites from the realities of
very difficult days. It made summertime special in Harlem. It was
an outing, an idyll, a musical offering, a retreat for lovers without
common shelter. Above all, Central Park was somehow both free
and elegant—a matter more of taste than of class.
     Most people think of Central Park as beginning at 59th Street
and ending at 110th. I always thought of it as the other way
around: it began at 110th and ended at 59th. I confess, our family
rarely got down that far. The feature show was the Mall in the
Concert Grounds where Edwin Franko Goldman played "music
under the stars" three nights a week; the other two nights found
him in Prospect Park in Brooklyn. The concerts were free, the
music was loud, and the audience (if you could call it an audience)
did more moving, eating, and ambling about than any other
audience I can recollect. Central Park was a proletarian paradise,
greenery everywhere in contrast to the gray cement streets, a place
to drive to nightly and leave behind the daytime woes.

I think my mother and father loved Central Park so much because it was as close to the old country as they were ever likely to get within the confines of Manhattan. Dilapidated housing gave way to grass, to flowers and trees in full bloom. Inside the park, everyone seemed to mellow. Friends would gather and gossip in Yiddish, Polish, Italian, Russian, Croatian, and Greek. There was no sense of imposing on others, or being imposed upon. Central Park was a private meeting place in a public space.

For me, Central Park was a vast school without walls—a place where learning occurred naturally. No teachers struggling to survive their pupils; no kids seeking to "beat the system" by not learning. Day excursions at P.S. 125 invariably meant Central Park. Because of its proximity to the school, these excursions were commonplace.

The American Museum of Natural History held a special kind of magic. From its Hall of Higher Mammals from Africa and India and the Hall of Evolution, I developed an awareness of how I fit into the long history of man and beast—not just as an external or didactic reality, but in the sense of inherent, never-ending struggle. One did not have to be a Darwinian expert to appreciate the degree to which we share a taste for combat and the will to survive with the rest of the animal kingdom.

And if other parts of the Museum seemed less worthwhile, then I at least found myself returning to this place of our animal ancestors again and again. This part of the museum was more interesting than the quiescent exhibits of Eskimos and Indians. These always struck me as idyllic and pacific to such a degree that the human forms seemed far less real than the gorillas and apes. It was, as I recollect, that massive painting of the gorilla beating on his chest, a veritable King Kong of a figure, that made me feel most at home in the natural museum. It became, for me at least, a social museum.

The Hayden Planetarium was a combination of *Star Wars* and *Star Trek*. I remember it as a new building—in fact, it opened only in 1935. The plush reclining seats made it hard to focus in the same way as at school. So, then, I came to realize, learning did not always have to take place on a carved combination seat and bench, bolted to the floor as if for all eternity. The show itself was spectacular. The heavens opened up onto constellations of stars and planets. One entered a brilliant universe—stunning, different, vast. There was actually life outside of Harlem! The toughest thing about the Hayden was going back out into the street. The adjustment to "reality" after such a special light show was jarring, even unnerving. What did all this mean?

It may seem odd, but the Hayden, dedicated as it was to a fusion of science and art, probably did more to stimulate my interest in religion than in either science or art. To witness the vastness of the heavenly panorama made thoughts about a divine order of things inevitable. To be sure, it raised heretical notions in an eight-year-old mind, so remote were these heavens from the austere and anthropomorphic gods of Christianity and Judaism. On the streets of Harlem, bodies would be beaten into the ground over the singular body of Christ; but in the Hayden, individual human gods were reduced to specks of objects rotating in time among gigantic forces that had no regard whatsoever for our puny moral judgments. All of these were private thoughts, of course. To share such heresies with Christy Roussopolous would have netted me a possible beating; to do so with Arthur Grumburger would have certainly resulted in a lecture or temporary ostracism. I've wondered since whether other children have walked away from the Hayden with simularly unsanctioned "learning experiences."

The other special place of the Central Park environment was the Metropolitan Museum of Art. The wonder that a boy from Harlem should be given such an opportunity to explore endless treasures of human creation on canvas, in stone, and in wood! What most attracted my attention at the time was the display of artifacts of European arms and armor. While it was designed to showcase an aesthetic achievement of the late medieval world, for me it was of a seamless piece with the Hall of Higher Mammals at the Museum of Natural History. For here, too, the emphasis was on struggle, combat, and weapons. Axes, maces, swords, rifles, even cannons—all seemed natural and fitting. While our attention was drawn by the guides and teachers to the design features of the weapons, my mind envisioned these marvels of intimate death and destruction as a perfect component of real-world struggles. I confess, with some shame, that in contrast to such tactile exhibits of Hobbesian brutality, the fine collections of Renaissance and Flemish paintings seemed very remote and deadly dull. In

Harlem, a real mace seemed so much more worthy a possession than a canvas filled with people doing devotionals and daily chores.

Visits to museums essentially took place during the school year. In this sense, there were two Central Parks: the pedagogic periphery and the entertainment center. The former was part of daytime and schoolday life, the latter belonged to the nighttime and summer existence. In truth, Central Park mirrored the city of daydreams and nightmares, of events light and dark—an environmental schizophrenia that was external testimony to my internal existence. If the Polo Grounds provided the outer limits of my world at the upper end of Harlem at 155th Street, then with equal veracity, Central Park provided another set of outer limits at 110th. Both represented the thrill of falling off the real world—of learning that the social world, no less than the physical environment, really was round.

With the exception of one bizarre episode involving Rex, my dog, the summers in Central Park carried very lovely memories. Learning music at school was a nightmare and a drag, but to hear the music on the bandstand was to know that "classical" music, the logic of emotion, was somehow connected to world emotion, to a divine order of things. The dignity of ordinary experience was reconfirmed on these warm summer evenings.

Central Park was also the place where I first saw large congregations of white people. It was a meeting place in a no-man's-land where for several hours each evening a strange mood of racial tranquility prevailed, adding to the unreal setting and the music. It was as if everyone understood Central Park as a special turf, a retreat from reality, especially the harsh realities of race struggles. Everyone involved in the social conflicts of the day could somehow take a breather and reconsider the world in the calmer, if not broader, perspective of the evening. During summer days Central Park was a barrier, a border, a definition of the sovereign limits of Harlem. But at night, it was an invitation to brotherhood—to a spiritual camaraderie of New Yorkers. And foremost were the Harlemites of the North (north of 110th Street at least).

My family continued to go to Central Park as long as we lived in Harlem. When we finally moved, the need for the place somehow vanished. Central Park is now so strongly identified with the wealthy homes adjacent to it, and with the hotels where the wealthy still live, that sometimes it's forgotten what a vital part of Harlem life it really was. Little wonder that it remains perhaps the most fiercely fought over turf in all of Manhattan. Who "owns" Central Park in the day owns industry; but who "owns" it in the night owns the soul of the city. This most public of places gave rise to my most private of childhood thoughts.

CHAPTER FIVE

Emotionally we are fluid, turbulent, tossed, our loves and
hates confusedly meshed. Unable to rid ourselves of the
guilts attached to ambivalence we can rarely take up any
one attitude or sentiment with complete conviction, to the
steady exclusion of its opposite. Without the "divine
word" to steady it, our emotional polarity remains in
constant uneasy motion, always reversing itself, turning
now one face upward and now its opposite.

Mezz Mezzrow and Bernard Wolfe, *Really the Blues*

Tom Mix

Saturdays were special. Between noon and 6:00 P.M. we entered
the magic world of the moviehouse, usually the Sunset, less
frequently the Alhambra, and at times the DeLuxe. They all had
in common an entrance fee of ten cents. The Sunset was best—
eight straight hours of unrepeated features. On the other hand, the
DeLuxe and Alhambra repeated their shows every four hours. At
the Sunset, you got twice the deal. True, the films may have been
two years old, or even older. But to a mind so young, no films are
dated. Cowboys are good, Indians bad, and the sagebrush smells
the same in a darkened theater. Moral verities change even more
slowly than plots of the "Western."

Another big advantage of the Sunset was the live show featuring
games of chance and prizes. Going to the Sunset was participating
in the glories of Hollywood itself; to win a bingo game and be
called on stage was an incomparable thrill—something like winning an Oscar or a Tony—a joy certainly not commensurate with
the junk given out as prizes. So Saturday was a crucial day not to

be tampered with. But there was always the same catch—the ten cents.

Finance was an area my father took strict charge of. My mother only offered vague moral counsel, using Russian buzz words meaning "give him" or "don't give him." Beginning Friday evening, my anxiety began to mount, reaching a peak on Saturday morning. I knew that even if I had been good, I still might not get the dime. This was Calvinism with a vengeance, with a Jewish twist—lemon in the soda. For the most part, perhaps three out of every five weeks, I did get the dime. Not so much because of my protestations, but because Saturday was a busy day for my parents: many locks to be repaired, window shades to be finished to size, keys to be made, bulbs to be sold, frames to be ordered. These things were better done in the absence of children, especially a nuisance child.

As I began to realize that goodness counted for less than the babysitting services offered by the Sunset, I also began to understand that wickedness had its reward. The earlier in the week I began to drive for the dime, the more certain it would be forthcoming. My every strategy was oriented toward that dime, including helping out with the inventory. My whole spiritual existence was wrapped up in that dime; it alone gave me the strength to endure the realities ahead—and behind.

On the Saturdays I got to go to the movies, I'd know an hour in advance. My mother would make me sandwiches to last through the day, and she'd smile a trifle more benignly than otherwise. That thin smile and those sandwiches were my tip-off. The only task left was to work on Eddie Jefferson and his mother. Eddie worked as a delivery boy for my father, so had some money of his own. He also had the advantage of not having my father in his house to act as ultimate arbiter. Eddie, too, would get the signal by virtue of the sandwich routine.

Those three out of five Saturdays were incredible days. There must have been at least six features, two serials that ended each week with the hero or heroine in trouble and miraculously recovering the following week. Then there were untold numbers of short features—everything from salmon fishing in Alaska to coalmining in West Virginia. But these were preludes to the main features. These had the main actors, the cowboys. There was Tom

Mix, Gene Autry, Roy Rogers, Johnny Mack Brown, Hoot Gibson, and countless other unnamed heroes in cowboy suits, as well as nameless Indian villains in feathers, and white villains in black garb on black horses. The highlights always came toward the end. By 6:00 P.M. we were all exhausted from the day's heroics.

The films had a narcotizing effect on us. I recollect always being stunned walking out into the daylight afterward. It was as if the outside world were an illusion, and the movies inside the realities being left behind. Everything about the Sunset thrilled me—the darkness, the solitary feeling, even amidst a crowd of other kids. Children held a virtual monopoly there. The adults were roped off in their own section for these Saturday occasions, as if they were some sort of interlopers, the way children are at adult movies. There was a tremendous cohesiveness in that darkness. Everyone's dreams blended into one; everyone's ambiguities faded in a world of perfect goodness. Victory indeed belonged to those who behaved righteously, and the inevitable triumph of good was at once thrilling and reassuring. We needed the reassurance that good would triumph; certainly it didn't on the streets outside.

Above all, the movies set Saturday apart from the rest of the week. Saturday meant life, reality, motion. The films, even the deadliest of them, touched my heart in ways that school never could. Saturday was a day dreams and nightmares combined in a singular, intensely private experience. Thus, to be deprived of a Saturday at the movies was more than a cultural deprivation; it was a form of punishment unparalleled in my young life.

When I grew up and saw Sergei Eisenstein's great epoch films, *Alexander Nevsky, Potemkin, Ivan the Terrible,* I was especially disturbed that his heroic Russians were dressed in black, whereas the diabolical Swedes and German hordes were cloaked in white. Eisenstein, too, had seen the cowboy and Indian movies; he was playing a practical joke on children of all ages ensnared by the bourgeois conscience. This transvaluation of film values saddened my recollections. To identify good with black and white with evil was more than I could bear; it was intolerable for a child of Harlem weaned on Westerns.

Of course, there were the two weeks out of five when the dime for the movies failed to materialize. Those Saturdays were days of weeping, of a deep sense of loss. A terrible note of discontinuity was struck, and events were out of synch. Just exactly how Buck Rogers got out of a burning spaceship, or how Dick Tracy foiled the thieves was never to be known. Missing chapters had to be reconstructed as you went from chapter seven to chapter nine. Little did I know that educational television would be playing these so-called great works of art thirty to forty years later. I confess I watched some just to make sure what, in fact, was in chapter eight those many years ago. We all fill in the missing parts of the past, but rarely with the authenticity that film reruns offer.

In these off-weeks when I didn't get the dime from my father, I had to play a game of cat and mouse with him. There were other ways of generating the dime, the most difficult and honest of which was through scrounging Pepsi and Coke bottles that were strewn along 125th Street. At two cents an empty, five equaled ten cents—and off I went to the movies. No sandwiches, but that wasn't critical. A simpler way was working the cash register. This could be done by hustling the customers. The movies didn't wait, so finesse was important. Putting me next to the cash register on Saturday morning was tempting the devil. Luckily for me, most of the time my father didn't know that I had worked the register; it usually cleared properly by the end of the day.

Stealing in Harlem was a way of life—an act of faith in the viability of the operating system itself. The test of character was doing so artfully, brilliantly, so that no one ever knew. An alternative to stealing a dime for the movies was to sneak into the theater. This was very hard to do on Saturdays; less difficult on weekdays after school. Many times Eddie Jefferson and I worked out an arrangement in which the fire alarm would go off at a prearranged time, allowing one or the other of us to gain entrance. We usually used the upstairs fire escape, which allowed less light to enter the darkened theater. Sometimes, on Saturdays, we arranged our entry to coincide with the live performance when light and dark contrasts were not quite as sharp. It's hard to convey how much we needed to get into that movie house on Saturdays. It would take the combination of a World Series game and Super Bowl Sunday to provide the same sense of urgency and need to put everything else aside. The movies, and what they had to offer in the way of entertainment and information, was the moral imperative. Impediments were just that, impediments. And ends and means are not neatly divided in the real world.

Even the best got caught, including me. On one occasion, an hour before movie time, my father caught me short-changing the register and pocketing the dime. At rare moments such as this, he became Moses and Calvin combined. There was neither mercy nor love. The pedagogical theory of punishment took over—education through beatings. On that Saturday my father was especially creative: "You want a Tom Mix? I'll give you a Tom Mix!" He used the laundry rope to tie my hands and feet to the hot-water pipe. My mother had gone out shopping that particular morning, so it was one-on-one. No match—my hands and feet were bound. The word *spanked* sounds so genteel, so perfectly bourgeois; beating across my bare ass more aptly describes what happened. I didn't know which hurt more—the heat from the pipes or the heat from the welts. In the movies, Houdini lurked behind Mix. But I simply couldn't undo the knots. I fainted.

When I came to, my mother and father were arguing. Not arguing—really fighting. They were shouting, screaming at each other, smashing everything in sight. My mother was not averse to punishing me either; but the difference between the two was in their sense of limits. My mother had a very clear sense of the limits of punishing behavior; my father simply lost sight of the harshness of the punishment. He unloaded all of his frustration, sorrow, and inability to make good in the new world onto me on those select occasions. He was more a part of the Harlem syndrome of frustration/aggression than he cared to admit, even to himself.

After that day, I never felt quite the same pleasure watching Indians being killed by cowboys in the movies, or even watching anyone being beaten or tied. Somehow the heart went out of my childhood experience of moviegoing. Fantasy turned into nasty reality. Of course, I still went; it was still an important event. Although I never stole another dime from my father, the relationship of good and evil remained cloudy for me. Growing up, itself, meant being confused as to what constitutes good and evil. On the other hand, rewards and punishments were perfectly clear. To be a child is to understand that distinction; to be an adult is to choose among goods and evils. In that sense, my father was more a teacher of moral development than the Sunset theater, although I wouldn't have admitted as much at the time.

CHAPTER SIX

North of 155th Street, near the Harlem River, is the Polo
Grounds, home of the New York Giants, National League
Baseball team. This stadium, built in 1912, seats about
sixty thousand spectators for baseball or football games.
Immediately west of the Polo Grounds, Edgecombe Avenue
climbs the crest of Coogan's Bluff and affords a view,
across the Harlem River, of Queens and the Bronx. The
vista is most sweeping from Roger Morris Park, on a rise
above Edgecombe Avenue between 160th and 162nd
Streets.
The WPA Guide to New York City

The Polo Grounds

The boundaries of Harlem were clearly defined, either by the
natural terrain or by human-made landmarks. The enormous
boulders of Morningside Heights separated Amsterdam Avenue
from Broadway. Central Park, which began at 110th Street, also
was a boundary. And in the north, the Polo Grounds both signified
the end of Harlem and set the boundary between black and white
neighborhoods. On the west was Riverside Drive, and on the east,
the Harlem River. The Polo Grounds provided the spiritual cen-
terpiece.

When I was eight, nine, and ten, the Polo Grounds was a place
for me to combine work and play; or rather work and delight in
watching others play. I had become a New York Giants baseball
fan late in 1936. Easy enough, since they were winners—National
League champs that year and again in 1937. Little did I know at
the time what a long wait it would be until the next pennant—the

so-called miracle of 1951 featuring the Bobby Thomson home run.

My devotion to the Giants could only be described as a love affair; going to the games was almost a religious activity. I knew everything about them—from their batting, fielding, and pitching averages to their personal habits. Baseball statistics became a way of life. Computing the batting average of a Bill Terry, the fielding percentage of catcher Hank Danning, or following the odyssey of Mel Ott from South to North became an obsession. Such computations were a lot easier then, since there were only eight teams in the National League and eight others in the American League. Given the fact that the hated Yankees were the American League stars, I wrote off that league entirely, at least until World Series time. The National League held out every hope, every promise. It was there, during a 154-game season, that everything of importance was determined. My then heroes were the above-mentioned Mel Ott, Bill Terry, and Hank Danning. They could do no wrong. Like Greek gods, they could be capricious—strike out or lose a game—but ultimately their heroics overshadowed their minor failings.

In the late 1930s, following a baseball team meant listening to the radio. Radio stimulated the imagination and made you want to see the game with an urgency unknown to the television generation. Baseball was not an escape or entertainment; it was life itself. But life has problems, and mine were twofold: I didn't have the money even to get to the ballpark, much less to buy a ticket. Getting to the game was the easier part to solve; it involved a long run from 123rd to 155th Street, straight up 8th Avenue. Getting into the game was the real problem. When a local policeman told me there were jobs available—specifically, working the stiles or, as it was known, becoming a turnstile boy—I was overjoyed. The thought of being able to see the games free—even be paid—was so extraordinary that it drowned out all my other thoughts. The minute the baseball season began, I participated in the turnstile world. For four or five years it became my exclusive summer occupation.

The turnstile operation was a management function. Management hired the personnel who sold the tickets in the booths and who officially received them at the turnstiles. These were regular employees of the New York Giants baseball club. But the boys who turned the stiles weren't management employees; the management took no responsibility for their health or welfare. The turnstile boys were hired by the New York City Police Department, which manned the stadium. It was a police sergeant who designated which boys would turn the stiles for that day's game. The system was modeled after the morning shapeup at the New York waterfront. For a 2:00 P.M. starting time, the boys would gather at 10:00 A.M. For a doubleheader, which began at 1:00 P.M., we assembled an hour earlier. This morning shapeup was as bizarre and nerve-wracking an experience at the tender age of eight or nine as one could imagine. Boys of all sizes, shapes, colors, and creeds were lined up, sometimes randomly, sometimes by height, sometimes by "seniority"—whatever that meant. The number of boys selected was partially determined by the number of stiles to be opened. If a heavy crowd was expected, more stiles would be needed and more boys chosen. But that basis for selection was only superficial. The real reason eluded me for a long time, and on those days when I wasn't chosen, I became very discouraged. The long walk back home seemed much, much longer than the short run up to the stadium.

The way the system really worked was to favor the "smart" turnstile boys over the "dumb" ones. What determined smartness was the ability to manipulate the tickets. The official rate of pay for the turnstile boys was twenty-five cents per day. The way to build up that amount was to participate in a minor scam. This worked best in general admissions; reserved seats were numbered. As a group of four or more people came in, the turnstile man would neatly palm one of the tickets and tear the other three. The closer it got to game time, the easier it was to palm a ticket. The untorn ticket was given to the turnstile boy who went up to the cashier and redeemed the face amount. The admission fee was $1.10. The split was three ways (that I knew of)—fifty cents for the ticket taker and ticket seller, another fifty cents for the policeman on duty and on the take, and ten cents for the turnstile boy. On a good day, say a Sunday doubleheader, the sting could be pulled off at least ten times. As might be expected, the boys selected to turn the stiles were extremely adroit at this maneuver and were chosen over all others in the pre-game shape up.

All this involved great finesse. Dumb turnstile boys, who had no idea of how the system worked, got to attend far fewer ballgames than those who were clued in. My first year, at the age of eight, I don't think that I handled more than ten games. But by the age of nine, in late September 1938, I had become entirely skilled. Under the educated gaze and guidance of the all-knowing police, and the adroit maneuvers of ticket-takers and sellers, one learned through observation the proper procedures for hustling tickets and fleecing the management. It should be noted that this learning process took place without a single word being spoken or a single question asked. The unwritten code was clear: intelligence was measured by what one could observe and translate into action, and not by the transmission of spoken words.

I sometimes wondered whether the team management had the vaguest idea of the number of stings that were going on at each stile. If the number of fans at a game was announced to be 52,000, you could easily say there were at least 55,000 fans in the stands that day. It was a system the police *had* to be aware of, and the way they selected the boys made clear their full participation in this plan for the informal redistribution of local wealth.

Once I was onto the system of working the stiles, my thoughts turned to the game itself. The stiles were shut down roughly half an hour after starting time, which meant I never saw a game from the start during all those years. My start was the third inning. I moaned and groaned at every crowd noise during the innings when I was at the stiles; and always I prayed for nothing eventful to happen. My favorite seating spot was between first base and right field, where I could watch Bill Terry and Mel Ott. Like every kid I emulated those players, including Ott's strange raised foot motion when he swung the bat. The hagiography was well known: a sixteen-year-old southern boy with a straw suitcase coming to New York City and asking Mr. McGraw for a job, whereupon he immediately becomes the starting right fielder without even minor league experience. There wasn't a boy in Harlem who didn't know that story or who wasn't sure it would happen to him.

The baseball Giants in those days were *in* Harlem but not *of* Harlem. They reflected an older era of Irish ethnicity tucked away at the outer perimeter of a black world. The heroes of the team were nearly always of Irish-American extraction. At that time, there were no black players on the team. The era of Willie Mays and Monte Irvin was yet to come. When the Giants were on the road, the New York Black Giants occupied the Polo Grounds. Since I worked those games too, I did get to see Josh Gibson, Satchel Paige, and other black greats of the time. Many games of the Black League were played in Yankee Stadium rather than the Polo Grounds. Watching the Giants against the Kansas City Monarchs was an awesome event in its own right. The lunacy of racial barriers was clear; as clear as the quality of the Black League itself.

In the fall there were also the football Giants. The old Polo Grounds was beautifully suited for football, far more so than for baseball. In fact, it was an awful baseball park with the strangest dimensions of any stadium: 250 feet down the right field foul line, 270 feet to the left field pole, and 510 feet to dead center, between the two clubhouses. But for football it was perfect, and in those days the football Giants and the Chicago Bears dominated. My football heroes of the day were Tuffy Lefmain, Mel Hein, and Al Blozis. But probably my favorite was the Bears quarterback, Sid Luckman. A paragon of Jewish-American success, Luckman combined physical prowess with smarts.

Reserved-seat tickets for football were $2.20 and $4.40. The same "sting" therefore netted twice the amount baseball did. Even in the late 1930s and early 1940s, the football Giants drew well. I was always sure of working. In fact, I can't recall ever not being picked to work the turnstiles for a professional football game. Even after I ceased working baseball games, I continued with football. It was only one day a week, basically five or six days in the autumn.

When people used to ask, "Where were you on Pearl Harbor Day?" I always knew. It was a Sunday, and the Giants were playing at home (I think against Green Bay). At about 2:00 P.M., it was announced over the loudspeaker that Pearl Harbor had been bombed by the Japanese. Some guy sitting next to me asked, "Where's Pearl Harbor?" I had no idea. No one else in the immediate vicinity did either. I'm not sure many people in the stands that day knew. After the announcement, the game resumed. It became just one more time out. After all, sports history was not to be interrupted by real history. Al Blozis who ate up the enemy defenses that day was dead two years later in the South

Pacific. But on December 7, 1941, the world was as normal as it had always been. Nothing peculiar or special, except the irritating feeling that I was getting too tall and too old to be a turnstile boy much longer.

Whatever the petty corruptions of the system, I had the thrill of growing up with live entertainment and a feeling for athletics that has never waned. On the small television screen, the panorama of a coliseum is diminished. I felt privileged to be at the ballpark. It was an egalitarian environment like no other. Quick friendships that lasted the length of a game, offset by quick animosities that were equally ephemeral. The rare, easy camaraderie that existed was based on knowledge of averages, teams, players—a universal discourse shared by young and old, which for all of its transitory nature was still a unique and acutely experienced phenomenon.

If the Polo Grounds was truly a world of careless joys, it was also a world of deep sorrows. The baseball Giants were to remain losers, as the Dodgers in Brooklyn emerged as the team of destiny. So we had to learn to lose, for we lost often and close. In retrospect, I'm not sure if it was the joys or the blues from which I learned the most. But in the constant presence of victory and defeat, I began to sense that the business of everyday living was more than a simple matter of rooting and shouting.

When the Polo Grounds was demolished to make way for a much needed new housing development, I felt a sense of sorrow; not so much for the loss of the ballpark as for all that this home away from home had come to represent. Living in a television era in which sporting events are private forms of entertainment only deepens that sense of sorrow. Now we can switch the channel and "tune out" as it were. Not so in the old days. A victory or defeat was a real-life experience that was shared with others. You carried it about you for at least a day, or until the next game. That's how life and games are really connected.

CHAPTER SEVEN

Americans have had an extraordinary talent for compro-
mise in politics and extremism in morality. The most
shameless political deals (and "steals") have been rationalized as expedient and realistically necessary. Yet in no
other country have there been such spectacular attempts to
curb human appetites and brand them as illicit, and
nowhere else such glaring failures.
   Daniel Bell, *The End of Ideology*

Hustlin'

The shapeup at the Polo Grounds was not the only way to make a
buck. To be sure, with only fifty or sixty working days the drive to
make money was intense. The turnstile experience was illuminat-
ing in many respects. Not only did I learn how tough it was to
make money, but also how important it was to figure all the
angles. After all, it was the hustling of tickets, not the legitimate
quarter for the day's work, that provided the "real" money—the
take-home tariff.
   My early lessons in money making were also instructions in
basic ethics, at least to the extent that I clearly understood how
getting caught carried with it severe penalties. The cash register
episode with my father convinced me that any move on my part to
go after the store sales was dangerous business. Being tied to a
pole for a day cowboy and Indian style was as close to actual film
making as I cared to get.
   So my first venture into entrepreneurship came well within the
parameters of legitimacy. It started with the Alfred Landon campaign of 1936. Not yet seven at the time, I knew little about

politics in American terms. About socialism I knew a great deal, in theory at least. It turns out that the local leader of the Harlem Black Republican Club frequented our hardware store—or at least had his keys and shades made there. So began the innocent deal that soon came to a nasty ending.

The ward boss asked me if I wanted to make some money on a Saturday. "All you have to do," he said, "is hand out these campaign buttons with the sunshine flower and the name Landon." This in exchange for one dollar for every thousand buttons handed out. It seemed easy enough. Indeed, inside of three hours, the deed had been done. True to his word, the ward boss gave me the promised dollar.

When I came back to the shop, the first thing my father asked was where I had been. This was no small matter, since on Saturday mornings I was supposed to help out by minding the shop. I explained what I had done, proudly displaying my dollar. At that point, my father did something I had never seen him do before. He took the dollar and tore it to shreds. My astonishment overwhelmed my dismay. This was as much money as we sometimes took in sales on an average day. More than that, it was my first legitimate earnings. "Filthy money!" my father yelled. "Contaminated." In his household, only Franklin Delano Roosevelt could be supported—and if need be, for free. Ours was a Democratic outpost; Republicans were all anti-Semites; worse, bad for the poor. Then with a hard slap across my tear-filled face, I was dismissed with a warning: "This will never happen again." I promised that it would not. Thus began my powerful identification with the Democratic Party. What we now euphemistically refer to as political socialization.

This experience with ward politics taught me several things. Not every legal form of work was ethically sanctioned; and also, not everything I did was to be reported to my father. These revelations stood me in good stead in my next adventure into the underground economy: as a bag-bog (known as bagman) for a numbers runner.

Actually, this was not so direct a negotiation. I was more a paid assistant to Irving the Cop. I was never privy to his last name (some things are better left unspoken) and I didn't know quite how I came to be recruited into so esteemed a profession in which honor is so prized. I do recollect being taken to the back of a black limousine. Frightened half out of my wits, I was interviewed by one black man, one portly white man, and Irving the Cop, whose "beat" was along 123rd Street and Eighth Avenue.

My task was simple enough. One hour each day I was to accompany Irving on his appointed rounds, come rain or shine, picking up the daily proceeds from the "numbers" that were bet each day. These could be bets on the final three digits in the parimutuel handle at a racetrack, or any suitable equivalent such as insurance premiums that could be objectively verified. The numbers would be matched to the cash receipts in some unnamed place (I had no idea where), and the next day I would be paid one-tenth of one percent of the handle. This amounted to a few dollars weekly—quite ample for my supplemental needs.

There were actually two financial transactions: picking up the daily handle and depositing the winnings with the same store-front proprietor for redistribution to those who chose the right numbers. Needless to say, enormous profits could be had. But this was far beyond my understanding. I did appreciate that I was never to look inside the bags (nothing more than small brown shopping bags), never to ask questions, and never to give answers.

The culture of the numbers game in Harlem was legendary. Winners were singled out to explain their magic, their karma. Tipsters produced sheets sold at small cost, offering advice on certain numbers to be played on certain days. Participation in such forms of gambling often swept whole neighborhoods. The poor were preyed upon, and they in turn preyed upon others, in the terrible game of survival and sustenance.

The time it took to negotiate each stop along the collection route was dependent on my quickness afoot. And with each passing day, my speed increased. I realized that this was an illegal activity; and I had no doubt that some people, many people, were being bilked out of their dimes, quarters, and even dollars. But I gave precious little thought to this aspect of the operation. The thrill of the gamble seemed ample enough reward for the bilking—or so I rationalized at the time.

Thus, at the age of eight, I did reasonably well in terms of my personal wants. No use in calling them needs. I had pocket money to buy candy, cake, and fruits. I could go to a movie house;

usually, on weekdays, Loews' 125th Street Theater. And I could do so without stealing—high status to be able to afford the purchase of such luxuries without having to resort to punishable theft. Indeed, the numbers game in Harlem was so enshrined that nobody considered it an illegal activity.

I had to use up the money I earned in numbers running relatively quickly. I knew nothing about savings, and having money that my father didn't know about seemed like a bad idea. If he found out, the inevitable beating wasn't something to be relished. Nor could I deposit the coins I earned into my school account, since my mother kept the bank passbook. This need to spend as quickly as I earned made the role of assistant to the bagman an ultimately unrewarding activity. In any event, within a year, Irving the Cop was reassigned, or so I was told, and I was cashiered out of my esteemed position. I never found out why the transfer for Irving, or why my own career loss. But I suspected that this was now a black job for a black kid.

For awhile, I was relieved not to have to make the daily rounds. Not because numbers were illegal, but simply because the pickups and collections had become a boring routine, taking me away from other after-school pursuits on the street. I also had become dimly aware that getting caught was a possibility. It did happen to others—at least so I was told. As an interim activity I sold newspapers. Essentially, this meant the *New York Daily News* and the *New York Daily Mirror*. The news trucks would roll around 125th Street at about 9:00 P.M. Independent vendors bought papers at three cents to be sold for five cents. My advantage was the ability to sell in front of our store. And on a Saturday evening in particular, most, if not all, the papers could be sold in three hours—sometimes less. The problem was that I had to buy a minimum number of copies to stay "independent." Otherwise, I would have to piggy-back my copies by purchasing from another independent vendor. I confess that all of this high finance was more than I could comfortably handle—especially since proceeds were in pennies, and my hours were limited, or so they seemed. There was also an element of dumb work involved. Selling newspapers was what nice boys did. Having already been initiated into the world of hustling, legitimate business constituted a serious loss of face.

After that brief interlude with petty bourgeois integrity, I turned to the poolrooms, of which there were plenty in central Harlem. I was back in my metier! I performed services on a catch-as-catch-can basis. If someone needed an errand run, I was there to do it—buying a racing form at the corner kiosk, holding side bets on important poolroom contests, and finally graduating into secondary forms of scalping.

It didn't take me long to realize that a ticket for a sports event had two values in Harlem: its face value and its purchase value. For major events at Madison Square Garden, the Yankee Stadium, or the Polo Grounds, a ticket could fetch a handsome price—sometimes double the face value. My turnstile activities proved very useful to my poolroom pursuits in that I could purchase advance tickets at the ballpark in accord with the wishes of the denizens and management of the poolhall on 121st Street and Eighth Avenue. Of course, there was a risk attached to advance purchases for resale purposes. But the level of sophistication of the poolroom denizens usually was adequate to the challenge.

They knew that a Sunday doubleheader of the Yankees against Cleveland or Boston would pack the stands. Likewise, nearly every game between the Giants and Dodgers would be sold out. My own role in this operation was actually legal—a relief unto itself. All I had to do was purchase reserve blocks of seats for special advance games.

These were purchased at face value, and sold by scalpers at twice or thrice that amount on the day of the game. Given the proximity of the Yankee Stadium to the Polo Grounds (one stop on the train or if I wanted to pocket the fare, a long walk over the bridge connecting Manhattan and the Bronx over the Harlem River) this was a small chore, for which I received a flat sum. It was only later, in my teens in Brooklyn, that I actually graduated to doing the scalping on my own.

Again, my own role in this operation was actually legal. I was given a token payment for these transactions. I also took it upon myself to find out how brisk were the advanced ticket sales—an important part of scalping, and much appreciated by my part-time employers. It was only later, and armed with the knowledge gathered from these experiences, that I actually did the scalping.

Harlem was a place of desperation: high unemployment, visible ownership of retail shops by whites (who often hired only whites as employees and salespeople), and black underachievement. It was a world of constant thefts, beatings, and hustles. The knife was the essential instrument of enforcement at the time. Guns were rare, and anyhow in short supply. In such surroundings and under such circumstances, where the victims preyed upon each other, doing anything on the street to "make money" seemed perfectly reasonable.

"Hustlin'" was factored into everyday life. Smart hustles were those who were not caught. Dumb hustles were those who were. It was as axiomatic as all that. But, still, other aspects of life prevailed. I still went to school every day. I still went to the hospital, to the park, and to playgrounds. It's just that I walked around, as did all Harlem kids, with an inner eye. Everything was to be looked at carefully—the crevice, the shortfall, the opening—the way to get something quickly for nothing; the search for some product that could be gotten cheap and sold dear. It was not so much a question of thinking, but of having—having what others had. And thus does poverty breed an ethic of entitlement.

There was no sharp distinction between working for something and hustling for someone. They were two forms of activity—each no better or worse than the other. Even my parents, concerned for my moral upbringing, explained a myriad of ways to price objects differently, charge various customers special rates, charge more for keys depending on circumstances, and even buy stolen merchandise under the right conditions. I will add that my father drew the line at buying merchandise stolen from his own shop, such as Chicago Ball Bearing roller skates. But that moral line was stretched awfully thin.

I can't recall any drug use or trafficking. I do recollect a big commotion about smoking. Cigarettes were viewed as a sort of elixir; an aura of illegality surrounded them. Smoking was also the singular mark of growing up. My sister started smoking at the age of seventeen and the commotion in the household was fierce. But all she was trying to do was figure out how to be an adult while living in a world of marginality.

I have the feeling that the criminal and moral climate of Harlem have changed little in the past half-century. I suspect that what has changed is the level of danger involved in failure. Using guns rather than fists, hustling skag rather than buttons, working against the cops rather than with them. Survival is probably much harder, and death rates among the young much higher. But the substance of the human exchanges are probably not all that different. It's hard to know whether to take pleasure in the continuity of culture or be saddened by the human lives sacrificed in that culture. I do know that hustling was a way of life ignored by the foolhardy, but also practiced only by the brave.

CHAPTER EIGHT

The Shepherd must and does exhibit a high order of
intelligence and discrimination involving the qualities of
observation, patience, faithful watchfulness, and even to a
certain degree, the exercise of judgment. . . . The German
Shepherd is not a pugnacious brawler, but a bold and
punishing fighter if need be. In his relation to man he does
not give affection lightly; he has plenty of dignity and some
suspicion of strangers, but his friendship, once given, is
given for life.
The American Kennel Club, *The Complete Dog Book,*
17th edition.

Rex

European Jews have a notorious fear of big dogs, especially German shepherds. I suspect that this fear is rooted in the same deep-
seated belief held by antebellum blacks: that these dogs are an
extension of armed authorities—police officers, parole officers,
prison guards. The Czarist police may have been less self-con-
scious about the breed, but no less aware of the dogs' potential for
maintaining law and order—otherwise known as keeping the
Jews in their place.

Not that I knew any of this as a boy. Indeed, and in all truth,
being one myself, I felt a kinship with every stray animal that
roamed the streets of Harlem. But there was no pet dog in our
house until I became eight years old. Not, I hasten to add, was Rex
given to me as a birthday present. Such niceties did not exist, as
should be clear from the episode of the Horowitz household's

vision of Christmas. Rather, my father thought it time to bring protection into the store.

With the enlargement of the store's facilities so as to sell basic hardware staples as well as service locks, windowshades, and keys, my father felt that a good watchdog was needed to deter crime. He also believed that a dog would provide protection for my mother when he was out and about doing odd jobs. The logic seemed right enough; what followed was something none of us could anticipate.

Enter Rex, a very large German shepherd, roughly a year old. My father assured us Rex came from a "farm in Pennsylvania"; more likely, he was a product of the Harlem pound. My father had a way of speaking of Pennsylvania as if it were a state very far away and, for the most part, rural. With the exception of one visit to Philadelphia (which occurred much later), I seriously doubt he ever saw the Quaker State. Certainly, unless the dog trudged hundreds of miles to find its way to the Horowitz household, the story of a farm animal was fabricated to shroud the true nature of the acquisition in needless mystery.

Rex and I became friends immediately. Each morning before school, and directly after returning to the store in the afternoon, I would walk him—ostensibly so he could do his business; in fact, as an extension of my power in the streets. Indeed, rarely did I feel safer on 123rd Street than in the presence of Rex. To tell the truth, he was never much interested in guarding; he was happier walking, running, and playing. But he looked imposing, and that was enough. Somehow, the pleasure I took in the dog unnerved my parents. In a household already laden with unresolved tension, Rex only made things worse. He did make my days pass faster, though, so intensely did I relate to him.

My father, perhaps reflecting the ambivalence of a Harlem shopkeeper wanting to preserve his life, and a Ukrainian Jew fearful of losing his life, had problems with Rex from the start. He was fond of saying that a dog must be put in its place, or more in keeping with the spirit of Frank Buck and Ringling Brothers, Barnum & Bailey, that a dog must be trained to obey, or else it becomes a threat to its master. Sometimes, when the going got rough, half out loud, you could hear him say, "It's either Rex or me." To my father, Rex was part of an alien jungle world—a lion or tiger, perhaps. In such a climate, the animosity between master and dog soon exploded.

Beatings of Rex, frequently with a long stick, became commonplace. And Rex, for his part, and in retaliation, never let my father come within paw's length without biting. It wasn't long after Rex arrived that he was chained on a steel leash (he bit through all others, and could open the links in softer metal). A circumference was drawn in paint, and this became Rex's private turf. My father dared not trespass on penalty of a bite. But in all of this fierce struggle, the dog remained loyal to me, and indifferent—but not harmful—to my mother and sister.

Because our quarters were cramped to begin with, the situation deteriorated rapidly once Rex arrived. It's amazing that he remained with us for nearly two years, from the summer of 1938 to the summer of 1940. But he did—unbroken, unbowed, but quite bloodied. Rex symbolized for me not just the ferocity of the breed; he became the embodiment of resistance to my father's hegemony over our small domain. He was the bark and the bite of resistance, even as the rest of us sat mute and terrified of the head of household.

None of this symbolism was lost on my father. He concocted a series of punishments to break the dog, and when all forms of physical mayhem failed to produce the desired results, he resorted to ways of "losing" Rex. He could not just destroy him, since within so short a time Rex and I had become fast friends, and he did indeed serve as some sort of deterrent to crimes on my mother and sister. But as the struggle between man and dog grew fiercer, the need for resolution became manifest.

The first attempt to lose Rex was in the summer of 1939. While an uneasy peace prevailed due to clearly delineated boundaries, allies and enemies were just as clearly marked, and my father found the situation intolerable. It happened that on Mondays and Wednesdays we often went to Central Park in the hot summer evening to hear Edwin Franko Goldman's "band." Actually it was a fairly large orchestra, or so it seemed to me at the time. They played excerpts (sometimes even full works) of all the greats, and the performances were free. This New York version of the Boston Pops for the Manhattan and Bronx proletariat attracted thousands of people. As I recollect, the same performances were conducted on Tuesdays and Thursdays in Prospect Park for the proletariat of Brooklyn.

We took Rex with us often, or at least as often as I insisted. He was always well behaved on such occasions, and much enjoyed running free through Central Park, rarely straying far and never getting lost amidst the thousands of people. Leash laws were lax if they even existed, and it seemed a good idea for the dog to get this special contact with trees and grass. My father could hardly object, given the "origins" of Rex on a Pennsylvania farm.

On the occasion my father determined to lose Rex, before the performance of the evening was concluded and during one of Rex's wanderings, my mother, Paula, and I were hustled into the car, whereupon we made our "escape" into the night. Of course, I realized instantly what was happening and beat at the windows of the car weeping and screaming. "Don't worry," my father said. "It's all for the best. Rex will find a good home. After all, someone in that big crowd will surely take pity and bring Rex home as a pet." "The dog is mine," I yelled. "He's my friend . . . you can't do this!" It didn't work. It fell on deaf ears. This was no random happening, but a planned attempt to get rid of Rex without taking responsibility for his actual death, and without returning him to the pound, where of course a fee would have to be paid—something my father wasn't likely to relish. My rage turned silent and bitter.

The last few minutes of the ride home were torture. All sorts of terrible fates crossed my mind as I imagined Rex consigned to the ravages of the city night. But as we approached the storefront, to the amazement of my father, mother, and sister, there stood Rex— panting for breath, but with that strange sort of smile that shepherds have in the sure knowledge of a triumph. As for me, my joy was complete. Not only had Rex found his way back home, but he had beat us getting there!

While the effort to get rid of Rex abated for the remainder of the summer, now it was my father's turn to become embittered. He had not only lost the battle to unload the dog, but he had done so in a way that exposed him to ridicule and further hatred. I was never again to trust my father or his motives; I was never again to permit any direct contact between my father and Rex if I could possibly help it. The return of Rex gave expression to my own deep frustrations: the desire to be free coupled with the need for a place of love. My identification with Rex had become complete.

But all this struggle for the mortal soul of Rex did take its toll. The beatings at the hands of my father made him especially fearful of long objects. And he developed some quirks, the most dangerous of which was dashing at people holding umbrellas. On a number of occasions when I was walking him, someone with a broomstick or an umbrella would catch his eye. This would trigger uncontrollable rage. Rex would break the hold and attack with alarming swiftness, often managing to bite his victim.

Now this was a serious matter. Dog biting man might not be news, but even in Harlem, it was illegal. Oddly enough, when complaints were made or filed, my father would settle the matter by paying the emergency room bills, if there were any, or by placating the victims in some other way. In retrospect, and without intending a lack of kindness, I think my father must have experienced his own symbolic revenge on the black Harlemites. After all, frightening the community was what Rex presumably was all about to begin with. That any connection existed between Rex being beaten with a stick and his ferocious response to long objects looking like dangerous weapons was vehemently denied by my father. Nor did he relish my bringing such a disquieting analysis to his attention.

The incidents became increasingly serious, to the point that local people grew fearful of coming into the shop to have a key made or a glass replaced. And in the loss of business, something had to be done. Clearly, the easiest solution would have been a cease and desist of violence done to the dog. But since this was not to be, Rex spent increasing amounts of time chained up in the back of the store—less and less happy with his circumstances, and with the moroseness dogs sometimes exhibit when planning their revenge upon the world, or master of the universe. In this case, my father.

That the dog had become a surrogate in the struggle between me and my father was plain. But this was no solution to the problem. An uneasy truce prevailed throughout the winter months. And it was not until the following summer that my father again took action. It came with my departure for a summer camp sponsored by Sydenham Hospital. Two weeks in the country for the ghetto poor is old stuff on the social welfare agenda. To be sure, the *New York Times* has been running its obligatory photo of the boys of summer camp every year for a long, long time. And every year I harken back to that tenth year when I went away— only to return to a home without Rex.

The summer camp experience was noteworthy for the number of white children I met. It was the first time I saw myself in a majority context aside from trips to downtown Manhattan. We were constantly reminded that this was a camp supported by donations from Eddie Cantor, a "sunshine camp." I confess, the experience was less than edifying or enjoyable. Rarely did I feel poorer, although I ate regularly; and rarely did I feel less free, despite being in the presence of birds and nature and all that. Regimentation was heavy: always what was "good for you"; always "for the sake of the children." Rest periods were mandatory, every waking hour was accounted for. And for the wild boy of Harlem, it all seemed too high a price to pay; better the hot cement streets and at least some degree of autonomy.

But if the "vacation" from reality was something of a letdown, the return to Harlem was worse. I was told by my father that Rex was gone. That he was back at the same Pennsylvania farm from whence he came. Naturally I realized that this was rubbish. But my mother sat stone-faced, my sister seemed indifferent—that is, she had her own problems with authority, beatings, and discipline. "You coward," I yelled at my father. "You waited until I went away to get rid of Rex." What followed was a long period of silence.

Indeed, this was the first of several periods in my life when my father and I didn't speak for weeks, even months, on end. We passed the rest of the summer in silence. I refused to go to Central Park, refused to eat on many occasions, wouldn't help out around the shop. I chose the path of passive resistance not uncommon to ghetto children. Every remembrance of Rex became sacred: the circumference that kept my father out, the food and water bowls, the steel leash that had come to symbolize resistance. My dog-friend had gone; a beast invested with the qualities of courage, yes, but an order of courage I myself invented to make the household tolerable.

Never again were we to have a major pet in the house. Parakeets and goldfish became the order of the day. Dogs were verboten. Rex was a singular event—a failed experiment for my father, a symbolic resister to me. But it was more than that. Rex was a living thing I could love and caress without concern. And if the words were all in one direction, the sentiments and feelings were not. When I grew up and read Sophocles' *Oedipus at Colonus*, I remembered with pain what one king said, and how it so deeply recalled the king of beasts who lived in my home of beasts: "I come to give you something, and the gift / Is my own beaten self; no feast for the eyes / Yet in me is a more lasting grace than beauty." And so the story of Rex came to an end.

But not quite. In one of those strange turns of fate, and many years later, the final episode in Rex's saga played itself out. It turns out that in 1973, when my wife, Mary, was working at Praeger Publishers, a co-worker of hers mentioned that some people from Brooklyn near Prospect Park had a dog they were willing to give away free to a good home. We had recently bought a house, and in a relatively rural environment we felt it might be wise to own a big dog who could provide the bark, if not the bite, that would lend us a sense of security.

This was on a Friday, and for some reason, I decided to invite my parents over for a car ride after supper. We would all go to this house in Brooklyn and see the dog available for the asking. So off it was, reminiscent of those childhood summer outings by car to Central Park with Rex. The house we sought was directly opposite Prospect Park, and true to the owners' description, this was a mixed breed with shepherd markings and collie fur and disposition.

The master of this dog was a store manager at a local A & P supermarket. He got the dog with the expectation of taking it out on Sunday morning hunting trips. The trouble is, was, that Patricia, as the dog was called, had no hunting instincts whatsoever. In fact, she was actually fearful of any sort of gunshots. No way could Patricia ever track other animals or lead her master to the quarry. So it was that she was free for the taking. But as fate would have it, Patricia shared a household with a young boy (about nine years of age), his older sister, and his relatively indifferent mother.

When Mary and I entered the household (my parents remained in the car), the scene was like a wake—the father wanting to quickly make the transaction, the little boy weeping bitter tears at the imminent loss of his friend. My spirits sagged at this terrible replay of a childhood scene. *Last Year at Marienbad* played in waltz tempo. I will say that the father seemed dumb, but not vicious. All the circumstances were explained, and the boy was even calmed down by the prospect that Patricia would have a "good home" with people who would care—nonhunters to boot. I promised the boy that he could call or write whenever he wanted to. And although I felt terrible at depriving the youngster of his dog, it was clear from the expressions on the faces of the other three family members that a fate far worse awaited Patricia if she didn't find a home with us. So it came to pass that within half an hour, the dog, together with her bowl, chain, and various licenses, walked out with us into the warm air and back to the car.

Now Patricia is not, was not, a Rex in gender or in size. She was smaller of stature and gentler of disposition. But she was part shepherd, which meant ferocity as well as strength. And on that first night returning to the car, Patricia looked every bit as imposing as Rex. So here we were, some thirty-five years later, replaying the story of Rex. Only this time, I was doing the driving and my parents were in the back seat. At the first sight of Patricia, my father blanched and sighed in disbelief. He let out an "Oh my God," or better, an "Oy Gott in Himmel . . . " and then lapsed into a silence that lasted all the way back home to his apartment in Coop City. No other words passed between us for the duration of the trip. None were needed. We both knew that Rex had returned, as a female, smaller and quieter, but with that same implacable set of characteristics that makes the shepherd a special sort of friend to special men—and boys.

As a postscript I should add that Patricia remained to grow old with us for sixteen years—outliving my father by several years, and never knowing that she was part of an old story of love and oppression.

CHAPTER NINE

The inhibition of the free play of emotion must lead to frustration. Human energies need outlets. If onstage acting does not allow for release of tension, then the escape should take place backstage. But what if there is virtually no backstage? . . . When masks crumble and crack, when people can no longer stand the strain of the front, then what we call nervous breakdown occurs.

Annabelle B. Motz, *The Family as a Company of Players*

The Jewish Family as a Company of Players

The ancient Greeks had in common with the Elizabethan tragedians a sense that the locus of drama was the family. But for such ancients as Aeschylus, Sophocles, and Euripides, and English classicists on the order of Shakespeare and Jonson, the families portrayed were dynastic in character. Gods and nobility thundered, raged, raped, murdered, and occasionally loved. The world of moral drama involved a cast of characters of sufficiently high status to justify such carryings on. In Jewish theater and novels, from Sholem Aleichem in the old country to Sholem Asch in the new world to Isaac Bashevis Singer who bridged both worlds, family life was no less filled with tumultuous events that tore at the

mortal flesh of all the members involved. But the people portrayed, unlike the larger-than-life characters in Greek and Elizabethan drama, were now ordinary people. Even the great
Chekhov, the father of Russian drama, created people who may
have been ordinary in emotional terms, but who at least were
empowered by wealth and a large measure of worldly comforts.
Not so the Jews. Even the most humble of them were involved in
the heroics reserved by other traditions and cultures for the powerful and leisured members of society.

This anomaly was deeply embedded in Jewish life. Survival
itself was bound up with family solidarity. The essence of communal life was a cluster of families huddling in some shtetl for mutual
protection. But with the coming of the immigrant generation to
America, conditions changed and values were transformed. Not
the necessity of communal life but the quintessential worth of
individual life became paramount. Jews who could survive cen-
turies of assaults on their very existence were finally confronted by
an enemy far more potent: the individual conscience, free to make
choices. Pluralism or Protestantism, call it what you will, sent
shivers down the Jewish spine and tremors through the immigrant
soul.

To be sure, one solitary family growing up in Harlem could
hardly be bothered with the architecture of culture writ large.
Such abstractions as communalism and individualism would have
been either ignored as perverse or hooted down by those who still
held firm to traditional verities: like father, like son; like mother,
like daughter. Likenesses were destined to continue across time
and space. But the breakup of communal life was precisely what
the Horowitz family had to confront as a single unit—along with
just about every other first-generation immigrant family coming
and settling in America. It struck the Jews with particular force,
since it threatened the very survival of Jewishness as a cohesive
doctrine structured to weather the storms of the world.

The Horowitz family saga is a single playlet in this larger drama
of American transformation. Perhaps the deepest tragedy of all is
not what took place, but that so few people (certainly none in my
family), had any sense whatsoever that they were shouting parts
whispered in the social cosmos. The roles they played echoed the
deepest instincts of Jews in the Western world. The trauma of

Jewish family life deteriorating was a necessary precondition to the Americanization process. The irony was that the players in each family thought they were performing unique roles and uttering personal lines of liberation never before expressed.

The stunning fact of life about Harlem was that the family was much less significant a factor than it has come to be (sometimes for better, sometimes for worse) in middle-class life. There was not much of a family around to either praise or damn. To be sure, punishment came much more readily than rewards. Anger became the common household denominator. The deterioration of family ties proved a blessing in disguise. Individual needs and wants displaced the authoritarian collective.

The essential factor about my parents, especially my father, was that he was much closer to the Russian peasant tradition than to the Jewish learned-man tradition. He was a man of action and was not especially reflective. He had golden hands but a somewhat less than golden mind. There is a tendency to mystify Jewish family life, to assume that every family from Eastern Europe celebrated the values of education, philanthrophy, and good food. In my family, these values for the most part were ignored.

How could it be otherwise? My father hadn't come to America so much as he had fled from Russia. He was the victim of the Czarist army in the First World War. Severely injured on the Austrian front (sustaining six bullet and shrapnel wounds and barely escaping amputation), he was ordered to return to the front even before he could get off his crutches. Once returned, he decided to flee. When I asked him what the final straw had been in his decision, he told me that when he had asked for soap and alcohol to bathe the wounds on his infected leg, his Czarist commanding officer had replied that Jews washed their wounds in snow, and if there was no snow, in dirt. Twenty-four hours later my father was on a long odyssey to the West. It took him first to Warsaw, where he connected up with his older brother, Moses, who had just married a Rumanian girl. From Warsaw they went to the port of Danzig, which at the time was under Polish and German occupation, not yet having been declared a free port. To emigrate to America required first a visa, second a proof of funds for passage, and third a ship's boarding card. The ship's card was essentially a boarding pass and was simply a number assigned on a first-come, first-served basis. As my father told it (later confirmed by my uncle), Moses dictated that the boarding passes be switched, that he should go earlier, in place of my father, being that he was both older than my father and, by virtue of his new wife, wiser. The boarding passes were transferable.

My uncle left Europe on Christmas Day, 1919—only lo and behold, it was in South America (Argentina), not North America, that he landed. It was a hot, sultry day in Buenos Aires and the skyline, while clearly metropolitan, was missing the famed Statue of Liberty. The weather was wrong, the skyline was wrong, and the language was wrong. My father, meanwhile, having switched cards to a later ship, ended up in North America on a cold, wintry day. In his case, the weather was right, the language was right, and the Statue of Liberty beckoned to its poor and downtrodden children. On such small administrative details hinged the fate of immigrant families.

My father was one of seven brothers. Moses went to South America, my father went to North America, and the other five remained in the Soviet Union. From the outset my father's condition in America was something less than a success story. He came to America without his wife—in fact they were not to see each other for eight years. He went to work as a tailor, but proved entirely inept at piecework. He then took a position as a union organizer in the Brown Shoe Corporation, then located in Providence, Rhode Island. More than once, he was nearly beaten to death by company gangs in the early days of ILGW organization efforts outside the New York area. From Rhode Island, he came to New York, where a series of increasingly onerous jobs awaited him. His salvation proved to be his skill in manual labor—he could repair anything from shoes to houses, build any sort of object from scratch, and do so with enormous skill. A tiny shop in Harlem was where his odyssey ended. There, he made keys and windowshades to order, repaired locks, and made and repaired frames. His reasoning for settling in Harlem was crude but not unsound: he chose the poorest area of New York with one of the highest crime rates because locks were constantly picked there, and windows constantly broken. Small tinkering was a needed skill. A new generation of blacks was even newer to the urban environment than he was.

My father designed his strategy more as a survival technique than as a means to accumulate wealth. He didn't have to work for others, and no investment capital was required. Certainly, he had none. In retrospect, I think that was a dominating impulse for my father: not to work for others. By temperament, training, and morality, he was not suited to work for anyone else, so firm was he in his conviction that he could do things better than anyone else. He may have been right, but right or wrong his approach was based on self-reliance, self-discipline, and self-help. He was the perfect Sombartian man—the Calvinist Jew, convinced that the road to heaven involved good work and no nonsense.

This aspect of self-reliance, this urban transcendentalism, was to cost my father dearly. He never could accommodate the needs of others. He never could tolerate shortcomings in others, and the idea of failure was anathema to him. By all reports, my father was a tyrant—as stern a taskmaster as Cotton Mather was to his children. Perhaps Werner Sombart was right in suggesting that the Jews were the highest contemporary expression of Calvinism; he was certainly right in sensing the tear between individual drives and community impulses to survive.

The problem, however, was that Harlem was the wrong place for a Jewish Calvinist. In America eight years by himself, without a woman (or better, without a wife), my father learned not only to live once again as a single man, but as a single man in a cosmopolitan environment. He was not above the usual hypocrisy— a stern moralist living the immoral life in a world of women amidst a sea of ethical imperatives to do otherwise. The grandson of a rabbi cut adrift from moral law; the son of a soldier in a world of urban guerrillas; an anti-Jewish Jew in a world of pious Christian blacks—my father's world had gone astray. All previous norms had failed him. He was trapped by tradition rather than liberated by modernism.

In a last desperate effort to recapture some sense of normality, he brought my mother, Esther, over from Europe in 1928. She was the idealized immigrant featured in the film of some years ago, *Hester Street*. She was unschooled in English, untutored in any discipline, and completely unaware of the new world that was to greet her. She arrived with her arm around a seven-year-old blond daughter, Paula, who had never seen her father. It was not exactly a scenario that augured success. In roughly sixty years of marriage, a peaceful day rarely transpired between my father and my mother. The resentments were mutual, and so were the penalties extracted. Two teenagers had married because of their splendid dancing techniques and their commitment to the ideals of Jewish socialism. Ultimately, and by their own admission, they became two people perfectly betrayed: my father humiliated by an immigrant wife, saddled with an immigrant daughter, and financially impoverished by the effort to bring these two to the new land; my mother enslaved and hopelessly trapped, unable to go anywhere or do anything or perform any services, especially during those early years surrounding my birth. Her English was halting and groping, her sociability reduced to mutterings. They were a pair of people caught in a swamp of poverty and deep isolation by virtue of my father's settling in Harlem. They were cut off from community life, other than the life of Harlem with its strange, sometimes frightening, argot. My mother and sister never recovered from their plunge into deep isolation. It was not so much a shock of recognition as a shock of not recognizing what Harlem, U.S.A., was all about.

My mother's first table was her suitcase. Her first meal was with relatives who gave both her and my father a different cut of meat than they themselves were having. Her first home was a small anteroom in the rear of a small shop. My sister, I was told by all who knew, was the absolute belle of the ball during her first seven years in Russia. A blond beauty revered by a large extended family in Europe; the perfect little girl with perfect habits, perfect playmates, and a perfect socialist future as a Komsomol in the brave new world of Soviet society. Photographs of her on a pedestal confirm her august place in the pantheon of family players.

Paula had no choice but to accompany my mother to America. Her first contact with her father was as with a stranger. Her schooling was postponed until her English was adequate, and then she was sent to Wadleigh, a vocational high school, a universe of black girls, a finishing school for poor girls. It was a school intended to equip young ladies with the basic skills necessary to earn a living, but they were given little sense of the world beyond the livelihood. There were few academic courses; most were "commercial" courses, as they were then referred to.

My birth was the first act of commitment by my parents to the brave new world. It was, like everything else that greeted these two people, a mixed blessing. The birth was painful, and it was at least twenty-four hours before my survival could be ascertained. From the very beginning, everything was a struggle for me. I was born to parents who considered birth defects in a child something to be ignored rather than treated; accepted rather than overcome. From all I can reconstruct, the event of my birth was neither a cause for dismay nor celebration, but rather was taken as a fact of life, the fulfillment of a commitment and an obligation to more suffering. I was a genetic heir to a Jewish tradition neither practiced nor preached by my parents; a biological misfit in a world of societal misfits; an impoverished child in a culture of poverty.

I inherited my father's life-long ambivalence toward Soviet power. In his case, of course, it stemmed in large measure from memories of Czarist persecution, together with an innate skepticism that any Communist ruler could be much different or better. Like so many other Jews from the Ukraine, he desperately wanted to believe in the Birobidjian solution—the conversion of a little segment of Russia into a new Israel; a land where Yiddish prevailed and where Jews were in charge. This also squared with a Socialist Bund position based largely on anti-Zionist, or at least non-Zionist premises. All of these sentiments were held against hard realities because it was convenient to do so. In this age of denunciation of Stalinism, we forget that socialist support had the distinct appeal to an immigrant generation of being pro-Russian, pro-Jewish, and not the least, pro-American. The sacrifices Zionist commitment required, with an implicit call to return to an historic Israel, were not easily digested by immigrant families. For my father, Harlem may not have been the new Jerusalem, but it was not the old Kiev either; and he was not prepared to risk his hard-won Americanization for a one-way ticket to Zion and Palestine.

And so it came to be that a series of beliefs, with hardly a shred of external confirmation, held sway. In this family environment, being Jewish meant something very different from the traditional Friday night seder. One could be Jewish and be modern, too. One could dress in everyday garb, denounce religious bigots in Jewish habit, and identify with socialism—the religion of the future.

How sad it is that such comforting syntheses finally collapsed on the shoals of everyday life. When it did so for my father, the impact was shattering: an end to political awareness or even interest. By the mid-1950s, he had become the recipient of canned television news. The maker and shaker of events he thought himself to have once been was dead and buried. Not even my mother paid him any heed at this level of political mutterings. The family as a company of players was gone. Only a shell of bare civility remained; and that's all there was until the bitter end—the deaths of my mother, sister, and father in the 1980s, in that order of removal from worldly cares or concerns.

CHAPTER TEN

If we once concede that traditional marriage, however flawed, could have some emotional life of its own—could indeed scarcely help having some emotional life and generating some kind of two-way relationship between husband and wife—then we ought surely to look at the connection between marriage and society *from the inside out*. Instead of marriage being a puppet show created by one huge, eternal, all-powerful masculine enemy, entirely for his own pleasure and convenience, we may begin to see marriage as an autonomous, natural and moral institution threatened and often oppressed from outside by a series of enemies thrown up by history.

Ferdinand Mount, *The Subversive Family*

Becoming
Self-Reliant

For as long as I can remember, the central aspect of the Horowitz family was the absence of love. It was easy enough to explain this away with the economics of impoverishment. But that was not quite a sufficient explanation. In the world of our relatives, especially among my aunt and uncle (the Schneiders) and their three daughters, there was no lack of warmth or affection or outward displays of love. Aunt Jennie and Uncle Isadore were no less in a state of impoverishment than we were, but they seemed far less burdened by this ineluctable fact.

Uncle Isadore, a fine and gentle soul, worked as a men's tailor and cutter in a garment industry sweatshop, in circumstances that seemed far more severe than the tiny entrepreneurial model my father was following. So why the great outpouring of affection in the Schneider household and not ours? Gifts were a big thing with them. They remembered every holiday and every birthday, and they used them as occasions to let me know that personal things mattered. With my family such things were overlooked. It seemed not so much a lack of love as a lack of symbolic resources to support such a concept. The small informal ways people let each other know that they matter—that someone cares—were simply not present in our subversive family. As a result, the harshness of the economic environment was translated into the harshness of the family environment.

From the outset, I built up a strong sense of self-reliance at the cost of social graces, and at no small cost in terms of interpersonal relations. The usual warmth people exhibited toward others became a danger signal. This helped later—in the inevitable break between offspring and parents—but it hurt in the beginning. There was not much trust to start with. I say this now without remorse or regret because, at the very least, I learned what it was to struggle. No rewards to be had simply for existing. Paula and I were given no preferential treatment on the mere grounds that we were daughter and son.

The most severe moments of trial came on those special days when I had to enter the hospital, followed by the day of the surgery itself. They were uniquely painful moments in which my loneliness was overwhelming; this coupled with a child's feeling of forlornness which, at times, was excruciating. I confess, notions of self-reliance failed to offer much comfort on such occasions. This is not to say that affection was entirely lacking; rather, it was more demonstrated than displayed. During my long hospital stays my mother, for example, did come and bring me supplemental foods—the proverbial chicken soup—that made hospital food more bearable. It would be wrong to say that I was totally without family resources. It was simply that the affection needed to sustain my essential needs was not there.

Because both my parents worked in the shop, I was raised more by my sister than by either of my parents. Having a sister ten years my senior was a great advantage. Paula, too, suffered the same lack of emotional nourishment at home. But somehow she was able to show me the affection that was not forthcoming from our parents. We had America in common, she and I—its musical culture, its politics, and its optimism. We spoke English not as a first language, but as an only language. It helped us separate ourselves from what our parents were.

I often feel in retrospect that our adolescent life was a conspiracy of two children against two adults. Paula taught me a lot of things my parents never could. It was she who took me to the Apollo and the Alhambra and who introduced me to popular music. It was she who brought dictionaries and encyclopedias into the house. And having herself become Americanized, she did the same for me. It was not easy for Paula to be both sister and mother to me and at the same time our parents' reviled daughter. But she served in such multiple roles admirably.

Paula suffered much more than I did at our parents' hands—if for no other reason than that she came first and was expected to provide a model of behavior. She was constantly punished for small things. Buying the *Times* on Sunday for ten cents rather than the *News* for five cents was likely to get her in trouble. Buying lipstick or other makeup was another source of tremendous friction, especially between my father and Paula. Once more the puritanical nature of home life coupled with the peasant harshness prevailed. Makeup became a terrible danger, a manifestation of the break between my sister and the household; it was therefore bitterly denied her.

Paula was not beaten often, but she was beaten; and those occasions had a great impact on me. The occasion I remember most clearly was when Paula brought home a black girlfriend from Wadleigh High School. Even though we lived in the midst of Harlem, and even though the patronage of my father's service activity was one hundred percent black, or close to it, no social interaction across racial lines was permitted. Bringing a black friend into our miserable dwelling was simply untenable. So Paula's fellow student (I think her name was Claudia), even though she behaved in an entirely normal way, was a cause of deep concern to my parents. That evening after the schoolmate had left and we had eaten supper, my father launched into a tirade over the dangers and awful consequences of interracial mingling. Paula was seventeen or eighteen at the time, and her social conscience was well developed. She totally rejected my father's position, arguing instead the need for everything from socialism to racial equality. My father's tolerance for dialectical reasoning was never very strong to begin with, and virtually absent when it came to his children. He beat Paula unmercifully. I remember how shocked I was—not only at the beating, but at the furniture moving about. And at my mother's impotence; worse, even ambivalence about what was taking place.

I don't want to give the impression that every day brought a renewal of physical violence behind our family walls. Most days passed calmly enough. Nonetheless, there was physical violence; and the threat of severe punishment hung over the household more or less constantly. The more I witnessed and endured, the happier I became that the embrace of love was not too tight; it made the violence easier to endure, if no less comprehensible. It was, at any rate, "normal" violence—traditional yelling, hitting, breaking things—unencumbered by sexual overtones and ambiguities.

About the time Paula finished high school, she suffered what was euphemistically referred to as a nervous breakdown. There were stays for her at Bellevue Hospital, Rockland State, and other institutions that lasted from two weeks to two months. Most of the time, she returned home after receiving some dosage of electroshock therapy. The years of Paula's life between the ages seventeen and twenty-one, and my own between seven and eleven, were filled with painful reminders that the family as a company of players was not the same as a Broadway musical and not quite the same as an O'Neill tragedy, in which lace-curtain people talk each other to death in anger and hatred. The consequences of family violence can be brutally direct. My sister surrendered and I resisted. From an emotional standpoint, she perished while I survived.

The state of the art called psychiatry was such that I don't recall either of my parents being subject to any questioning or even interviews. It was taken for granted that the "patient" was Paula and that the cause of her illness rested solely with her; never with society. What was so terrible about that circumscribed view was that it managed to avoid dealing with the culprits. Shock therapy became the cure. But all that really resulted was a deepening pattern of violence and depression, leading only to additional rounds of shock therapy. The end of the process witnessed not the cure of a person, but the disintegration of a personality. And there was not a soul around who could articulate so simple a condition. The only one who could have, my sister, had been deprived of that capacity by her so-called curative treatment. An eerie quiescence became her silent fate.

It's not easy to describe family life without scorning it, without exaggerating the pain endured or minimizing the normal routine of everyday existence. It was a long time before I understood (perhaps I never quite will completely understand) the roots of our family violence—or, not much better, emotional neutrality. For my father, Paula and I were unwanted intrusions, mouths to feed, obligations, limitations on his movements—impediments. My sister suffered doubly, as a hangover from an old world, a connection he couldn't sever, and as an organic linkage to a wife he could no longer love—if, indeed, he ever did.

From his point of view, America was a tantalizing land that at once announced and betrayed his every wish and expectation, not so much because the promise wasn't there, but rather because the realization of that promise was so elusive. The source of his frustration was externalized—the family itself—the immigrant wife, the immigrant daughter, the disfigured native-born son. All this was much too much for a man of limited horizons to begin with. Physical violence as a norm was a predictable release from frustrations that in his mind could never be resolved.

For my mother's part, there was a sense of hopelessness in response to the violence. There was also ambiguity, since the perpetrator, my father, was also the source of her security—what little of it there was in the new world. I suspect my mother felt betrayed by the new world, not because she had any grandiose expectations; quite the contrary. Rather, it was that all the familiar landmarks of language and terrain had been removed by virtue of her immigrant status, leaving her with a very limited ability to make any choices. By the time choices were permissible for her, she was either too old or too frustrated to make a move. The norms of the age were against separations and divorces. There was an almost animal-like faith that family "solidarity" was better for growing children than a broken home. In this emotional context, my mother persevered with a bitterness toward my father that became increasingly manifested late in her sad life.

It was only when, by accident, she found out that my father had amassed a small fortune (at least by pre-World War II standards) that her alienation from him became complete. For a woman denied all but the bare essentials of life, whose clothes were essentially hand-me-downs from relatives who presumably had more, this discovery was more than she could carry. My mother could live with the idea of poverty, of struggle, and even of failure. But the discovery that money had been available throughout the Depression—that the endless rounds of screaming and cajoling for a chicken on a Friday evening, or for a new print dress for a Sunday outing, had been unnecessary after all—utterly destroyed her equilibrium. I don't think I ever saw her smile, much less laugh in the final years of her life. Her face seemed frozen into a sardonic, twisted grimace. She would have been better off without discovering how well off we really were and had been for a long time. That revelation, I suspect, caused her to die a few years earlier than she would have otherwise.

I mentioned before that the coldness of my family life was not without substantial advantages. It toughened me and made me self-reliant very early on. It also provided an emotional freedom to pick and choose my friends and make them all the more important parts of my life precisely because affection and love were so limited within the family circle. To be sure, I couldn't always bring my friends home, but that did not seem to matter so much. The boys of Harlem lived on the streets more readily than did the girls. The lack of family comfort made me aware of others in a special way, forcing me to seek friendships in a world of my own. All of this helped ease the pain of family wounds.

Living in the kind of family that I did, there was little time for self-pity, or for reflection on my infirmities. One learns early on that every human has infirmities. Only in my case they showed more plainly. Given my situation, any sort of reflection would have prevented any step I took toward normalcy. As it was, life was severe; I dreaded, for example, those moments in classroom encounters when I would be called upon to speak, since they brought forth giggles and catcalls. How could it have been otherwise, with the severe speech defect I had at that time? But curiously, the very fact that I couldn't run home and cry on my mother's lap forced me to tap all my inner reserves and resolve to speak better to solve the problem; to do what had to be done to survive.

The parental technique (if one could call it that) in dealing with my infirmities was simply to deny their existence or their preeminence. Fortunately, the doctors had better means. But every time I came home in tears, my parents were somewhat bewildered, as if my tears were absurd, as if all the other children should have been the ones to be scoffed and laughed at. In itself the technique was frustrating, but again it threw me back upon my own resources time after time; and in everyday situations I found the resolve to copy this parental denial of reality ready at hand. What else was there?

As I grew into adolescence, the family scene counted for less and less. Paula lived a life increasingly devoted to work—sometimes to hospitalization, sometimes to boyfriends (some good and some not so good), and finally to a marriage that was not so good, but like my parents', long-lasting. With her removal from the circle of family life came my own removal. Because Paula was a surrogate parent, her absence from the home removed the parental support, but also the parental roadblocks. By the age of ten, I was quite thoroughly on my own, a streetchild of no mean prowess.

My parents in the meantime were busy expanding their tiny operation to find a niche for my mother within the confines of the little shop housing frames and glass and keys. Increasingly, a retail hardware line was brought into the repair shop: electrical lightbulbs, pots and pans, and kitchenware of all sorts. My father remained the tinkerer, my mother became the retailer. A hilarious mismatch internally. Two less likely people to run a retail shop in Harlem could hardly be found. Their small income was indicative of their ludicrous situation. The role they played in my life continued to diminish. Pure and simple, a street urchin was what I was. The family as a company of players had completely dissolved. There was no great show of victory on my part, no great defiance. After all, no significant battles had terminated the war. It had been, rather, a slow erosion of the very meaning of family life within the Horowitz household.

If the family Horowitz dissolved as an emotional entity not with a bang but with a series of cries and whimpers, it could hardly have been otherwise. There was too much going on in the life of the community—at school, hospitals, and among friends—to draw my attention. My parents lived at their best and worst, in a world of Russian folk music, the Yiddish language, and above all, peasant habits of mind and thought. Mine was the world of the native American—of school, of English, of politics. The political life somehow seemed interesting. Breaking the linkages that bind never quite took place, because those bonds, supposedly so characteristic of Jewish life, were never there to begin with. Our entire extended family knew that ours was different precisely on that count. It was a last, deviant, peasant outpost rather than a new Jewish emancipation in America. It was only later, after meeting many other people and families, that I better understood how different we were.

My parents, too, in their own tormented way, came to understand the deep lack of cohesion in our family. My sister had two children (a boy and a girl) and I had two also (two boys)—and my parents lavished great affection and attention on all four. There was an outpouring of genuine love for the grandchildren. Perhaps this was a making up for all the tragedies and bitterness that had existed in our own household. It could have been a genuine effort to show they felt remorse. In that curious generational stage-skipping, the humanity of my parents reasserted itself, and long after the family had become a series of fragments, their decency was restored. Putting behind me the bitter memories of those childhood family scenes finally became possible—not by reconciliation, but by stage-skipping. Perhaps this is the hidden secret of the bond between grandparents and grandchildren.

CHAPTER ELEVEN

Meaning is conferred by processes of social interaction—
by people. Such is the case with children. Each generation,
each social group, every family and individual develops
different interpretations of what a child is. Children find
themselves defined in shifting, often contradictory ways.
But as a sense of self is acquired, the child learns to
transport from situation to situation a relatively stable set
of definitions concerning his personal and social identity.
Indeed most of the struggles he will encounter derive from
conflicting definitions of selfhood and childhood.
  Norman K. Denzin, *Children and Their Caretakers*

Children's Secrets

Children live in a world of children. This is probably the simplest
and hardest lesson for adults to learn. Grownups want to believe
in their own godlike power for much longer than it actually lasts.
In the case of our family, the world of other children became
important and unobstructed mostly because neither of my parents had the time or the inclination to play God, at least in a loving
sense. This was because God is smitten by the middle-class America, and my parents were not. There was little love given; and
hence, as the saying goes, little love lost or withdrawn.

  The bonds of relationships with friends were quickly broken
when we moved from Harlem. These were powerful bonds, and
nothing was ruptured more painfully by virtue of departure. The
thought that of my three closest childhood friends two are dead
and the third disappeared—never heard from again—still comes
as something of a shock. The problems of living and dying pene-

trate the world of Harlem in a very special way, perhaps because life is lived so intensely and the urgency of dying is never remote.

As I mentioned, three children in particular were important in my growing up. First, there was Arthur Grumburger, known to me as "Grumpy." He was the son of Hungarian Jewish immigrants who owned the haberdashery shop on 123rd Street. Then there was Christopher Roussopoulous, simply and aptly nicknamed "The Greek," whose parents owned a modest diner at Hancock Place. Finally, there was Harvey Cropper, otherwise known as "The Bopper," whose mother was a seamstress who worked at home. Harvey's father I never met since he wasn't living at home at the time.

Grumpy had a younger sister, Alice, who died at the age of six from what was described as an enlarged heart. Her death was my first encounter with this nightmarish subject. I knew something was wrong because Arthur spent several evenings at our place and Alice was gone by the time he went home. Alice was extremely bright and the only girl I knew as a friend until adolescence; that is, until I left Harlem. Because of her infirmity and because I was slightly older, I shared my schoolbooks with her. She always ended up knowing much more than I did. She taught me by asking smart questions. I don't believe she ever set foot in a school in her brief six years on earth. I remember her only dimly as blond, small, and always sitting up in bed—never walking but invariably smiling. It was her death that cemented the friendship between Arthur and me. In truth, there was more to divide us than to unite us in terms of personality. But his was the only other Jewish family around. Our friendship was made inevitable less by common concerns than by the shared fears and doubts we could whisper only to each other beyond earshot of the two sets of parents.

Arthur didn't attend P.S. 125; rather, he attended a Yeshiva, a private Jewish clerical school. Also unlike the rest of us, he went for full days, not half days. Our days ended at three, his at six. Still, our interaction was intense, and often took place in the context of the family—his family. That first friendship started out as a series of denigrations and humiliations: Arthur knew everything about geography, stamp collecting, religions of the world, and for reasons I never could quite fathom, air power. I suspect that the last item derived from an early appreciation his father instilled in him for the military might of German Nazism and Soviet Communism alike.

Arthur carried in his head the make and vintage of the airplanes at the disposal of every major European power. He was also an excellent chess player; his father taught him that, too. He gave me a taste for stamp collecting, geography, and military power all in one large bite. He also opened my eyes to religion. Every learning session was painful, constantly reminded as I was of the Grumburger family superiority versus the utter, hopeless inferiority of the Horowitz family. Grumburger-the-Elder, Milton, did little to disabuse such feelings of cultural chasms, since he viewed my father as a heathen, my mother as a victim, and my sister as a tart. Arthur's mother, Ethel, on the other hand, exhibited no such feelings of grandeur. After all we were all locked into the same block in the same corner of Harlem.

The relationship between Arthur's family and mine was indicative of a larger pattern. Jewish immigrant families seemed far less concerned about external threats to Jews as a whole than about relative advantages of one ethnic variety of Jew over another; in this instance, of Hungarian Jews over Ukrainian Jews. Every display of ignorance on my part only confirmed the Grumburgers' sense of superiority. Still, denigrations and all, the Grumburger family and Arthur in particular opened up worlds that I could hardly have imagined otherwise. Nothing in school had nearly the impact of his unlikely trio of interests. The most serious moments came on Friday nights and Saturday mornings, when I was taken by the elder Grumburger to the large temple on Riverside Drive. While my parents never objected to this, they didn't particularly support it either. They were happy for the respite, but not quite certain of what it meant to go to temple in the Harlem periphery. For my parents, the synagogue was deeply and darkly reminiscent of European oppression, whereas for the Grumburgers it was with equal passion a mark of Jewish survival. What it was for me at the time was awesome—the biggest building I had been inside of, and the quietest. I had a sense of being in the presence of a magic God and contrite subjects; a religion without Christ, a church without crucifix. This aspect of the Grumburger family I took to less well than collecting stamps or playing chess. Nor was I quite sure what the military power of European nations had to do with temple worship. We were all to find out in the immediate years ahead. In retrospect, I know old Milton Grumburger, with his air of self-satisfied condescension, knew more about the world of politics—the real politics of survival and death—than did my own father living in the imaginary world of Jewish Bundism and Russian Bolshevism.

Arthur himself, as I was to find out in later years, had his own doubts about Jewish orthodoxy, but he kept them well hidden. He was truly an alien-looking creature in our Harlem world: wiry to the point of being bony; tall, but poorly coordinated. One would have had to say homely in the extreme. He insisted on wearing his *yarmulke,* and he had long *peyes,* or sideburns. He was a boy who marked himself apart and was so marked by others. And in the name of an identification with the collective fates and fortunes of traditional Jewish people, he was nonetheless more of an individualist than the rest of us children combined. It took guts to be so self-identified; and while I privately mocked his beliefs, I knew in my heart of hearts that such put-downs had a great deal to do with my own timidities.

One pays for being different in a subculture of difference. Arthur was victimized in ways I never knew or cared to find out. He fought poorly, but he cried never. He had courage of a sort that even his enemies envied. It was the courage to be beaten up and to keep on fighting. I don't recollect Arthur ever winning a fight, but I don't recollect him ever giving up. In many ways, I grew up with an image of Judaism fixed by Arthur—by his tenacity and willfulness and, at the same time, his inability to develop any strategy other than to lose. I was filled with admiration for his courage and loathing for his infinite capacity for defeat.

For the Grumburger family, being Jewish was far more important than being in favor of socialism or making a living; it was the organizing principle of family life. It was this core element of the Jewish tradition that our family never experienced. Yiddish was an important embellishment that set us apart—but not so much as a positive culture; more as an immigrant culture—an inheritance we carried about, like so much old baggage. It puzzled me how people like the Grumburgers could have such a strong affinity for Judaism as a religion with scarcely a nod in the direction of Yiddishkeit as a culture. How it fit together, what unified such diverse people, I could hardly understand, much less reflect upon, in the hubbub of daily life in Harlem.

It was probably too much for Arthur as well. When I managed to get together with him years later, when we were both in our late twenties, he had left the religious calling in favor of becoming a biochemist. We accidentally met at City College and, of course, immediately recognized each other. Several years later, Arthur's job cost him his life. He was working for the Sewer Department of the City of New York and contracted a fatal disease while testing the city's water quality. That the Grumburger parents outlived both their children is, in itself, a terrible thought; one that intensifies the near-comic tragedy of dying in a New York sewer. But before his death, Arthur had made his peace with the world. He had become more at home with the everyday romance of life and less concerned with the exotic aspects of living. Both of us had long ceased collecting stamps, but strangely enough our interest in everything else, from air power to theology, had remained intact; Arthur Grumburger—nervous, frail, and insolent—was the source of such enthusiasm.

Christopher was another case entirely. He had been thrown out of parochial school and dumped at P.S. 125. Being that he was the only other white kid in attendance, once again the friendship we shared was one of convenience. It's hard for me to imagine two more different types of kids than Grumpy and The Greek. Christopher was extremely handsome, a well-built boy with incredible physical prowess. We had a teacher in second grade who would measure her power by how quickly she could make children cry. If the tears came fast, or if at least you could feign crying, no real punishment came your way. But if you held out, heaven help you! There was no doubt Christopher would use every occasion to torment the teacher and make life miserable for everyone else. But when it came time for punishment, he was in a class by himself—quite prepared to pay his dues. The teacher had an eighteen-inch ruler with a metal edge, and she would apply a rapping of knuckles commensurate with her need to make a child cry. Christopher held back the tears, smiled through the bloody knuckles. Asking him why he didn't complain or why his parents never came to school always produced the same response: the teacher was right and, besides, it would only make matters worse to complain since his parents believed that was what school was about anyhow—discipline. Christopher never became disciplined. He recognized but couldn't absorb lesson one of Harlem school life.

Christopher imbibed all the values of a small white enclave in Harlem. It boiled down to a matter of turf. If his physical courage in the classroom was formidable, it was no less so in the streets. Every day, Monday through Friday, was warfare time on Morningside Heights. And every day Christopher was there. The war between whites and blacks began at 3:15 P.M., precisely a quarter hour after class let out. It lasted until dark, roughly 5:30 to 6:00 P.M. in the autumn. The other children in the white enclave knew that Christopher remained an outsider. His friends were from the local Catholic parish close by Hancock Place. Ambiguity set in. Kids like me—Monday through Friday—were white like Christopher. But Friday night through Monday morning I was magically transformed into the "kike"; the enemy of all things Christian and sanctified. Somehow Christopher readily navigated this world. Oddly enough, so did I. To each other—abstractions aside—we remained friends until the end, until he and his family moved to Pennsylvania Dutch country, or so I was told. Why a Greek father and an Irish mother would move to Lancaster County remains a mystery to me; but that was the story I was told and the story I accepted.

Christopher taught me many ways to fight and survive: run if you could, climb fences, defend yourself when you had to. Christopher never lost a fight. It totally astounded me and still does in retrospect. That a white boy could have such an extraordinary passion for fighting and do so well at it against black boys went against everyday experience. That it was even possible to win filled me with awe. The model of Grumpy, of losing, still remained strong.

Christopher was a good teacher. But faced with the choice of fighting and winning or fighting and losing, I began to think, or at least hope, that there might be a way to avoid the fighting altogether. Not that I harbored any grand pacifist convictions as a child. Confessedly, I had none. Rather, it became evident that to survive it might be smarter to negotiate situations than get killed or do the killing. It was a lot easier to lose a pair of skates than a set of teeth. I also took full advantage of my quickness afoot; whenever it was possible, I ran. I couldn't quite understand what it was that Grumpy learned from getting beaten so often, or what Christopher was teaching when he was doing the beating. But I had plenty of time during hospital visits to reflect on the madness of street life and my two strange white friends.

The story of Christopher would be incomplete without mentioning our frequent discussions about religion. By the time I was ten, going to shul with the Grumburgers had become part of my routine. I had even developed a sense of what it meant to worship. In the Roussopolous household over each bed there was an enormous crucifix. When I confessed to Christopher that this artifact frightened me, he replied that it should—that was its purpose. It was large to remind me that the Jews killed Christ. So essentially I was labeled a killer—at least a symbolic one. This coming from the toughest kid I had ever known didn't do much to calm my fright. But I did ask Chris why, if he was such a hot Christian, he beat up on blacks and they on him; after all, weren't they all Christians? It was from Chris that I received my lessons on the black children of Ham. Chris had answers for every question. They were all predicated on the superiority of being white and Christian and resolving all problems that might arise between races or religions in such boastful terms.

It would be a mistake, though, to think that Christopher and I spent very much time in theological disputation. He was a wonderful kid, a good friend, and a great benefactor and protector. He exempted me from all the sins of my forefathers, and he in turn was someone I could hardly imagine being on the other side of any barricade. He was delightful, spirited, and physical: the Greek ideal counterbalancing the Hebrew prophet represented by Arthur Grumburger.

Harvey Cropper represents a slightly later stage in my life. I was already ten or eleven when I first met him. He took a job at our shop once a week on Saturdays learning how to make keys, fix locks, and do other odd jobs to help out my father. The racial antagonism among schoolkids was so intense at that time, that it took something like this forced interaction to break it down. Harvey was a special person. He had a dimension that neither Grumpy nor Christopher possessed—a worldliness and sophistication that the other two couldn't have imagined. He also knew music—loved music—and played the bass very well.

In Harvey's apartment, it was nearly always dark. When I asked him why he didn't turn some lights on, the answer was, "Electricity costs money." His mother worked as a seamstress by the light of the window. She was always very kind and slightly curious about me. It was a pleasant but poor apartment, dominated by musical instruments. The linoleum floor always squeaked when you walked on it—a constant reminder of genteel poverty.

I was not musically ignorant. By the age of ten or eleven I probably went to the Apollo Opera House more often and with greater verve than Harvey. No question that the basis of our contact was contemporary jazz. It was a kind of undercurrent—a game. I don't think Harvey ever acknowledged that a white musician could play music well. For my part, I never failed to mention every great white musician I knew. It struck me as odd that he knew these musicians but never acknowledged them as first-class. Black nationalism was the wedge that separated us. The question is still open as to whether jazz is a "people's music" or whether it belongs to any particular group, except in terms of origin. What part European? What part African? Can you separate out the melody and the rhythm? Harvey and I couldn't explore these questions with any degree of comfort. Who we were got in the way.

Harvey may not have been my closest childhood friend, but he did represent a transition to adolescence. It was he who taught me how to smoke; he who taught me there was a thing called marijuana. Harvey was my first real music teacher. It was with him that I went to my first parties. And it was through Harvey's cohort that sex became dimly real. Harvey's friends were much older than either of us. When he and I were alone, our interaction was intense; he was the teacher, and I was the willing pupil. But in the company of others, I simply admired Harvey's sociability, frustrated by my lack of same. His was a world that was strange to me—one in which even at the age of ten or eleven partying meant something special. My life seemed so much more prosaic than his; emptier, less filled with people. He enjoyed his popularity, navigating with apparent ease through the world of adolescence and all its complex problems. I never could figure whether Harvey befriended me simply because he worked in my father's shop, or whether he derived real enjoyment from my company. I certainly must have seemed an odd character to him with my knowledge of jazz, odder still for the academic quality of that knowledge. Harvey played jazz, I analyzed it; Harvey felt jazz, and I examined it. But through it all, for the last three years of my life in Harlem, he was my most important friend. It was his sensibility and prideful vision that formed my sense of Harlem as a unique place. He seemed so sophisticated and at home there. Arthur and Chris for their part seemed more like aliens. They belonged to a world of primitives—the Grumburgers with their fundamentalism; the Roussopoulouses with their bigotry. In comparison, Harvey Cropper was urbane and cosmopolitan. He belonged, and I envied the comfort it gave him. There was a knowingness about everyday life that he possessed, and that I desperately wanted to learn.

Harvey navigated the transition to adulthood, but never made it there. Later on, at City College in the late 1940s, I met a few friends of his. Harvey actually lived on 135th Street, right below City College, at the time I knew him. His friends told me he had died of an overdose of drugs. I never was able to confirm this, but it seemed reasonable enough. It wasn't that Harvey took drugs to prove the need for a high, only because it was part of the world of daydreams that afflicted Harlem in a special way. Drugs were not nearly as central to everyday black life as wine or whiskey. But for the younger, sophisticated black Harlemites, drugs became the mindlessness of choice. Drugs were also part and parcel of the music scene. And whether one played better under the influence of marijuana mattered less than being an insider. The rest of society was "out."

Harvey embodied my strange state between daydreams and nightmares. No realities, no work, no school—only music, parties, good conversation, and far-out friends. They listened to jazz and extracted meaning about sex and rebellion. The very absence of talk about world politics, the very nonexistence of a larger white world, somehow enlarged their sense of community; for want of a better term, racial pride. I was the invisible white boy in a world of budding black men. The learning experience was awesome, but so too was the deep hurt at being excluded so thoroughly.

Moving broke all my childhood patterns. It severed all my growing-up relationships. The black world of Harlem became the white world of Brooklyn as if by magic. Jewish children were no longer marginal outsiders; instead, they abounded. Here, the Christian kids seemed out of place in the mainstream of daily life. Friendships were formed in relation to school, shooting pool, and playing basketball. In Harlem, what bound the kids together was the common thread of survival. The lesson of the streets was survival; neither school nor community counted for much. Friendships meant everything; they were the key to survival. In the less angular world of Brooklyn and later, the Bronx, survival took different forms; no less serious, but certainly less purposeful. I came to view Harlem as a series of history lessons—for which Grumpy, The Greek, and The Bopper paid the ultimate cost. Neo-Darwinian doctrine may make for a few tough survivors, but in Harlem, at least, it extracted its price in many young and promising lives.

CHAPTER TWELVE

I truly had not realized that Harlem *had* so many stores until I saw them all smashed open; the first time the word *wealth* ever entered my mind in relation to Harlem was when I saw it scattered in the streets. But one's first, incongruous impression of plenty was countered immediately by an impression of waste. None of this was doing anybody any good. It would have been better to have left the plate glass as it had been and the goods lying in the stores. It would have been better, but it would also have been intolerable, for Harlem had needed something to smash.

James Baldwin, *Notes of a Native Son*

Armageddon

On the day following the riots, the mayor, Fiorello LaGuardia, urged calm. Black church leaders reminded the citizens of Harlem of their patriotism while looters were busily engaged in trying to sell merchandise stolen the night before—often back to the original owners. My father was offered a dozen pair of Chicago ball bearings at a fraction of cost. But the decision had been made, the die cast years earlier. The Harlem riots simply accelerated the exodus for the few remaining whites.

The closest Harlem ever got to World War II was on that post-riot day. It was as if the area had been bombed, and left so desolate that it couldn't possibly be put back together. The riots were our personal Coventry. The curious fact is that World War II changed little in the streets of Harlem. Too many men were still unemployed; too much tension remained in the *geist* of the place.

Shopkeepers were the visible enemies. For black militants they were the devil whites, for other blacks, Jews ascendant or ghetto profiteers. The "merchant of Venice" had come to Harlem. The chemistry was ripe for rioting. World War II brought an end to depression—everywhere but in Harlem, or so it seemed.

Everyone had an opinion as to who or what was to blame for the riots: maybe the Harlem Trade Union Council, or the followers of Marcus Garvey, of Father Divine, of Daddy Grace, maybe the police harassment of black soldiers home on leave. Or it could have been the inevitable outside agitators: the white communists, the black fascists. The plain fact was that the Harlem riots, like most riots, came about more through the absence of organization than its presence. With nowhere to turn and few places to go, the Harlem community turned upon itself, committed an act of immolation—clear for all to see in the desolation of the shops. The community itself had been badly ruptured. Chain stores left the area, small shopkeepers followed, and servicepersons—who fixed window panes and repaired locks— vanished. The Harlem community was left in charge of itself. It was a self that turned out to be an empty shell, at least for the duration of the war.

Although the riots seemed dramatic and sudden, the prelude to the storm had built up over years. We saw it all on 123rd Street and Eighth Avenue. The corner drugstore had folded and was gone; the Grumburgers' haberdashery likewise exited six months later. Cushman's bakeshop had been sold to an independent—but the cakes and breads were not of the same quality; nor was the block. My father had already made inquiries about work in the defense industry prior to the riots. As soon as the dust-had settled and the final bills were paid (to his credit, my father would never have thought of leaving with bills outstanding), he accepted a job at the Brooklyn Navy Yard as a third class mechanic's apprentice. The end of an era was all about us; the riots simply sounded the final knell. They reminded everyone that the war against the Germans and Japanese didn't quite blot out the war between races and religions at home. Long-standing American problems remained intact, albeit in limbo, waiting to be stoked by world peace and the triumph of the democratic order over fascism. Gunnar Myrdal's *American Dilemma* was a prescient indicator of what the postwar environment was to bring.

The riots came at a good time for me—between elementary school and high school. Thus, the decision of where to go was made *for* me rather than *by* me. Not that I cared much, anyhow. School was something of a veiled shadow. I can't recall any tremendous exhilaration I derived from it. It was partly the constancy of my surgeries and hospitalizations that prevented school from becoming an overpowering concern. And it was hospital life rather than schooling that served to link my Harlem past with my Brooklyn present. I still went to Sydenham for the final series of operations, even after we had already moved. Surgery was the last formal link with Harlem and with adolescence.

Looking back, it's easy to romanticize; especially in the case of a Harlem childhood. The fact is life was bleak—petty and boring, sometimes cruel. We all lived in the streets, not in the tenements. We shared a world with boundaries that were repeatedly violated, but boundaries nonetheless. We shared the ghetto, and the arguments were over who was worst off, not who was making it. My father and his neighbors would go back and forth over who had it worse in America—Jews or blacks. Here they were, mocking and reviling each other, all for the honor of being listed at the bottom of the stratification pile. The poor never had it so good. The riots became a consecrated monument to years of this sort of interaction between Jews and blacks without community, without shared affection, without love. Indeed, in public discourse this was all viewed as a black-white confrontation; but those of us who lived through the events of the Harlem riots knew better.

Blacks needed a spiritual capital in America. Harlem was the inevitable choice for the New Jerusalem. It had the rich and the poor, the cultivated and the uneducated. It became the Holy Land, a home for the rootless, the center of everything. For Jews in Harlem, there was simply no more place. Jews were beginning to discover opportunity in the wider world. Prejudice was real, but slowly it was breaking down. The Jew could get a haircut and a hotel room in any city in the country. Not so for the black. Harlem was the only assurance of that same haircut and hotel privilege. The arguments about being furthest down were thus settled by events, not by theories.

But this is all in retrospect. At the time, I saw Harlem as a trap; something to escape from. My familiarity with conversational Yiddish got me at least as far as the Sholom Aleichem School at the edge of Harlem at 125th Street at Broadway. In the year before we finally moved, I managed to get further. I discovered the joys of the nickel subway ride to any part of the New York paradise. Going downtown to the Paramount, uptown to Fordham Road, or to Brooklyn and Coney Island held all the thrill of world travel. Often, I went by myself; Paula had discovered the joys of her womanhood, leaving me in the lurch. For the most part, I jumped the turnstiles, but I rarely got caught. The city subway system took me to all parts of the city; my imagination took me the rest of the way.

With the Grumburgers' move, Christopher's migration to Pennsylvania, and the new exclusively black circles in which Harvey Cropper was making his way, I became a teen-age *luftmensch*. I learned the importance of traveling alone and traveling light. I hooked up with a Harlem poolhall that "gave" me tickets for scalping purposes. Again, most of the events were at Yankee Stadium, the Polo Grounds, or the old Madison Square Garden—places close to, but essentially beyond, ghetto walls. Thus, when the denouement came, it came naturally. I had already discovered the city and its delights. I returned home to Harlem later each night, with a sure knowledge that I would soon escape.

The end was unmistakable. I didn't go to school on that eerie Monday morning after the riots. Instead, I went with my father to the shop to estimate the cost of the damage and to see if any merchandise could be salvaged. Aside from a few locks and some key blanks, there was nothing worth saving or selling. But, after all, the truth of our Harlem existence was my father's labor power. The goods, in themselves, were of little significance. The riots only served to proletarianize my father—make him aware of the possibilities of laboring without the petit bourgeois illusions of a storefront. We surveyed the wreckage and with a few tears my father simply announced, "It's over. We move on now." And so it came to pass.

Although I quickly became absorbed into the general thrust of Brooklyn Jewry—new friends, new schools, new hopes—I never could quite shake my Harlem upbringing: a Jew with heavy traces of a black sharecropper's accent; a kid whose thoughts were more on hustling than on schooling. I continued to listen to WWRL, "the voice of the sepia people," long after I left Harlem—indeed, long after I left New York City as a young adult. My volatility was more frightening than impressive to my schoolmates. I was as lonely, lonelier, in the white world than I had been in the black.

I was asked a few times whether I had been bar mitzvahed. The answer was, yes, of course, but the truth was rather more painful. Unlike most other Jewish children, my rite of passage came not in front of the extended family and friends on a Saturday morning, but on a weekday morning in a small, local congregation, where barely a minimum number of congregants—a *minyan*—was present. Orthodox Jews, who feel that the occasion of bar mitzvah should not be reduced to a ritual of gift-giving, often have their children bar mitzvahed during the week. In the case of my father, however, no such pious reasoning was involved. He hardly ever went to synagogue—not even on the High Holy Days. What was at stake, in fact, was the usual economics. We simply couldn't afford a grand bar mitzvah. Then, too, my father didn't have to come to terms with the painful fact that his friends were nonexistent, and his family barely on speaking terms with him. Beyond that, and what grieved me most about the occasion, was that my father was embarrassed by my nasality and cleft-palate condition. Although there were still several important operations to come, he viewed it as an insurmountable impediment. I had the distinct, disquieting impression that the weekday service was a way for my father to hide me out while still performing a ritual so sacred and fundamental to being Jewish that not even he dared violate its sanctity.

My Hebrew was rudimentary, based on less than one year of occasional study. But the years spent in learning Yiddish were not in vain. The event went off without a hitch, but the feeling of deep humiliation, of receiving something less, much less, than Arthur Grumburger received, never quite left me. Not even my mother was present for the occasion. She had to mind the shop. It was, after all, a weekday, and that meant a business day. The ceremony was capped by a chocolate milkshake (my favorite), and I went back to school for the afternoon session. It wasn't so much a move into manhood as a passing out of childhood.

More important to this transition than the bar mitzvah were the riots. They occasioned the move from Harlem, an entry into the ordinary world of immigrant Jews and their offspring in Brooklyn and the Bronx. In short, a rite of passage that was as much physical as spiritual. It would be years before the old habits learned in Harlem faded away: a quick tongue, and quicker feet. The mode and style of Harlem—abrasive, combative, and angry—had penetrated my soul. And if I were odd boy out in Harlem, I was surely odd adolescent out in Flatbush and then the West Bronx. But that's a story for another time.

In Brooklyn, the need for community pulled us toward a more thoroughly Jewish environment than any I had ever known, or am ever likely to know—unless I migrate to Israel for my last years. True enough, things fell apart in Harlem. But they came together in a new form that transcended the orbit of family feuds and childhood friends. The end became a beginning, and the daydreams and nightmares of my Harlem childhood gave way to the more normal existence of youngsters in my station and class. Beyond black and white were boys and girls; beyond good and evil were truth and error. Beyond the extremes were the middles. The sages were right; childhood things had to be put to rest.

I left Langston Hughes no less than Sholom Aleichem. I followed the new releases of Ella Fitzgerald and Fats Waller much more than the croonings of Bing Crosby or Perry Como. My attitudes toward conflict and confrontation had already been formed. Reading Hobbes, Darwin, and Marx was no mere literary exercise; it was confirmation of the struggle for survival. The social solidarity others spoke of seemed terribly remote upon leaving Harlem.

During my years at City College, the walks along Convent Avenue and the dashes through Morningside Heights always reminded me of my origins. Moreover, I felt equipped with a sixth sense about the city as a whole, privileged in a world of impoverishment. If this sense failed me in the world of intellectual niceties and prevented an early polish, the worldliness that comes naturally to all children of Harlem more than made up for it. The block was the world. One escapes Harlem the way one leaves a prison: hoping never to return. But the stripes of the prisoner and the Harlemite remain. A spiritual osmosis takes place when the stripes of a confined life are woven into the fabric of mind.

CHAPTER THIRTEEN

The problem of the common schools in a democracy has reached only its first stage when they are provided for everybody. Until what shall be taught and how it is taught is settled upon the basis of formation of the scientific attitude, the so-called educational work of schools is a dangerously hit-or-miss affair as far as democracy is concerned.

John Dewey, *Freedom and Culture*

Movin' on Up

Emotionally, the move away from Harlem was gradual. But the end came so abruptly, induced as it was by a riot rather than a plan, that it seems fitting to describe what happened during the transition year. After the destruction of the shop in Harlem, my father went to work in the Brooklyn Navy Yard as an apprentice machinist. This was probably the happiest and most fulfilling of his experiences in America. He was able to put to good use his amazing ability to repair and tinker and replace. He was able to work in the context of a war effort—for an America he had come to appreciate, if never to know. And the fact that America was in a common struggle with Russia gave him a sense of communion with his relatives in the old country.

We lived not too far from where my father worked. Actually, it was quite a trip, but the BMT subway line was fast and relatively safe. And so it came to pass that we moved from the depth of a Harlem despair to a tranquil, middle-class neighborhood in Brooklyn—to 1269 18th Street, between Avenues "L" and "M"—

two blocks from Ocean Parkway and not far from the major shopping center of King's Highway.

When I returned there for the first time several years ago for dental surgery, the physical environment seemed pretty much the same, but I perceived it differently. Our apartment house which seemed so big during my adolescent years, so impressive, was in fact a very modest building that would now be called a low-rise. Russian Jews still live there, but they're new arrivals from a post-Stalinist Russia, rather than old arrivals from a post-Czarist Russia. *Çà plus change* indeed!

In that first year in a Brooklyn classroom, I learned quite a bit about the process of "acculturation," so termed in the jargon. For ghetto children, civility doesn't come easily. But school is, in fact, a process of becoming civilized, even against one's will if need be. All the talk of schools as breeding grounds for revolution and social justice notwithstanding, their essence is better explained by the religious authorities with whom early schooling was identified: a process of accommodating to the needs and the ways of the world.

Now, as I said, coming from Black Harlem to Jewish Flatbush was no simple matter. My name may have been Horowitz, but my behavior was clearly not in tune with that of the nice Jewish children who went to P.S. 193. For me, and I dare say for most of my fellow students at P.S. 125, school was a temporary restraining order from the joys of everyday street life; a period of the day in which adults were permitted to go about their business unmolested by the young. Also, at P.S. 125, I never thought of myself much as an individual. I was white, Jewish—more a sociological category. On the other hand, at P.S. 193, individuality counted for a lot. Each student stood out as a special entity—a person in his or her own right.

Maybe this was more true of the boys than the girls. The girls all wore white middy blouses and ties, and they all rolled their hair into a bun. This sameness of appearance detracted from their individuality, at least on the surface. The guys were less circumscribed by a dress code. Anyhow, I knew them better: Marvin "drink your milk" Waxman, Leon Hochberg, Richard Feder. The back of my graduation picture is filled with signatures—Stanley Kramer, Irwin Odell, Peter Flanagan, Gerald DiManno, Rosalin

Marcus, Amelia Pustigiacone, Alice Dinerstein, Donald Dugan, Kenneth Mayer, James White, Ellen Kaplan, Irene Varone. For most, I can still match up the name with the face. At P.S. 193, I came into my own. But the art and craft of becoming a person proved very painful. It was easier remaining a category.

I grew up in Harlem believing that school was a temporary respite for adults who needed to get rid of the kids for awhile in order to attend to the worrisome details of grown-up life. I used to think that after three o'clock the adult world shut down. It never dawned on me that the rhetoric of school as a learning experience, as an academic environment, was in any way positive, or that adults sacrificed and paid taxes to make schools happen. No way. School was a place you went to be kept from doing mayhem; lectures and lessons were incidental. And I'm willing to bet that most of my Harlem buddies shared this view with me.

At P.S. 193, words mattered far more than fists; finesse and cleverness were valued more highly than blunt and dirty talk. You went to school happily, not for fear that truant officers would go ratting to principals or parents. The Deweyan revolt against educational formalism never quite made it to central Harlem, where it was supposed to work its wonders, but the pragmatic ethos certainly prevailed at P.S. 193. No doubt there was more "freedom," but for someone like me it was an opportunity to work the system, not join in the fun.

On the first day of school, each child was given a civic duty. Mine was to direct traffic during comings and goings. That meant working at street crossings in the morning, at lunch hour, and at the end of the school day—four times a day directing others. Given my background, I was doomed to failure. In no way was I ready for the authority invested in me. I reacted to every display of disobedience with physical force. I pushed, and often I got pushed back. When all this degenerated into fighting, I was taken to Mr. Gewirtz, the principal. It happened again and again. Somehow, I had a hard time understanding that such incidents were to be reported to those higher up, not dealt with directly. The concept of a chain of command made no sense. I was the police and judiciary rolled into one small bundle of terror. Just like it was in Harlem.

Mr. Gewirtz eventually gave up on me—much to my pleasure, I admit. I was reassigned to hallway duty, which meant keeping the between-class flow of children moving on the stairwells without incident. Again, it became apparent that I was not suited for this type of work. The same brusqueness manifested itself, and it was not long before I was labeled a bully, or worse, a misfit. I had to be relieved of this assignment, too, in the face of numerous complaints—a few, even, from outraged parents.

I knew very little about sex. About what it had to do with love, I knew nothing. In Harlem I had seen a lot, but never understood what was going on. Of course, I knew that males and females were biologically different. And somewhere along the line, probably through Paula's beneficent intervention, I learned the sexual functions of the various parts of the anatomy. But despite my relative ignorance, by the age of fourteen, or at least post-thirteen, I was ready to try out what I had seen many times in Harlem: a man on top of a woman, or pressing her against a wall, heaving and rocking in rhythmic fashion. It was quite surrealistic—an act that mannequins could perform.

The "act" I remember most vividly from the Harlem period was the one I saw take place between a man and a pregnant woman. She was obviously, unmistakably, pregnant, belly bulging like a watermelon. I was shocked that a woman in that condition could or would engage in sex. What added to the shock was that I'd seen this same man making it with other women. So I seriously doubted that this one was his wife. The event made a deep impression on me. I was convinced that that was the way to do it—tough and quick. Terms of endearment never entered into my picture. Of course, you had to say some nice words, but this just was part of the hustle. This was all I took with me from Harlem with respect to sex education. And at P.S. 193 it stood me in very bad stead, indeed.

During my brief tenure as stairwell monitor, I became enraptured by a girl. Every morning she came down the stairs at the same time. I waited for the moment, fantasizing about her body. I wanted to introduce myself to her. But how? I had neither the charm nor the finesse of the other boys. And my reputation as a bully, earned right off the bat, didn't help the situation. This girl was probably scared stiff of me—that is, if she took any notice whatsoever.

After two weeks of watching and waiting, I saw this girl in

relatively uncrowded circumstances—away from her usual cohort of girlfriends. This was my chance—one not to be missed. King Kong meets Fay Wray! I grabbed the poor girl and slammed her against the wall, just as I remembered from Harlem. I tore at her clothes, tried mightily to kiss her, at the same time yelling profanities—all of this without even knowing her name. Naturally, she was terrified, and I became very frightened, too. I wanted to soothe her, to show her I meant her no harm. And indeed I didn't mean her harm. But neither did I know what to do. I had no idea of what an erect penis was to do, where really it was to be inserted. Suddenly it had become an embarrassment—a betrayal of my deepest emotions. And after a few more heavings and sighings, I let the girl go. Everyone else on the stairs was staring in blank horror. No move was made to rescue the victim, no move made to stop me. It was all so surrealistic. I was playing out a schoolkid's fantasy, violating a taboo. But I was doing something—anything—to count, to matter, to connect.

This was not Harlem, and such incidents as molesting a girl didn't go darkly into the night. My parents were summoned to school to be confronted by the parents of the girl—who by this time was far more fearful of their wrath than any permanent damage that might have been done to her body. Indeed, I vaguely recollect a glint of satisfaction more with me than with the punishment meted out. It was agreed that I would be prohibited from attending class for two weeks and, in the event of any repetition of such behavior, a school official would contact the police department who would "have me fingerprinted"—no doubt relegating me to the common-criminal class. I recollect the girl's parents claiming that all sorts of "diseases" might have been transmitted, from pregnancy to syphilis. Although the thought of walking around with the power to transmit babies and illnesses at the same time warned me off girls for the remainder of the eighth grade, I kept wondering why Harlem kids seemed to manage sexual intercourse without incurring the wrath of parents and other authorities. The white world was certainly different.

As for my "punishment," I could barely understand it. What was so bad about being deprived of going to school? Wasn't that the goal of playing hooky? Wasn't that the aim of all normal children—to escape the drudgery of school? The officials must have gone mad. Did they really think that suspension from school would be a corrective to corrosive, antisocial behavior?

Well, in fact, it did work that way. I missed being around the other kids. My suspension turned out not to be from school but from class. I had to report each day to the office of the principal, and I would sit in Mr. Gewirtz's corner not permitted to talk or to leave save for going to the bathroom. But in some strange way, that two-week suspension was a learning experience. I saw how things worked from the perspective of a principal—a person handling endless rounds of complaints and calls about sicknesses, misdemeanors like smoking in the bathroom, small lies, small thefts, small symbolic murders.

I began to see myself in more lifelike, less heroic proportions. For the first time, I recognized myself as the problem. And the ways of the streets couldn't provide answers. Brooklyn wasn't Harlem. Not every issue had to be resolved physically. There was something called equity, some justice, some fairness. Adults were not mere dispensers of authority; some—Mr. Gerwirtz—had wisdom. My departure from Harlem began to acquire psychological meaning, no less significant than geographical distance.

The long, slow process toward civility had begun. There were others, besides me, who collected stamps. There were others who had an interest in the war and in politics, generally. There were others who enjoyed playing sports. And all of this without an unbridled passion or for purely selfish reasons. The idea of learning as an end in itself became important. School didn't mean an escape from others, or even from myself. I could talk to girls without attacking them. All of this seems so elementary—the kind of things you learn in kindergarten. But it took the riots of Harlem and the ruins of a war to permit me to learn the ordinary, the routine. Essentially that meant learning from other children, no less than from teachers. These kids were united in common pursuits that were constructive, not destructive. Teachers weren't enemies—at least not always.

It's not that the world turned rosy as whites replaced blacks and Jews replaced Gentiles in my everyday world. To the contrary, life became more complicated and harder to cope with in everyday terms. Still, I recognized, almost instinctively, that new opportunities beckoned.

One very important incident in this regard was a confrontation with Mrs. Mims over the nature of Communism. Since these were war days, and the Soviet Union was the ally of the United States, classroom discussions about Soviet power did not seem out of place. Indeed, with Mrs. Mims, they were always in place. On one such occasion, when the virtues of the Soviet regime were being extolled in what I thought to be excessive terms, I complained that I thought the Communist system was a dictatorship, with all the rules made at the top and followed at the bottom. For good measure, I added that the Nazis and the Communists had no trouble making pacts before the Soviet border was crossed.

Mrs. Mims did not take kindly to such subversive talk, certainly not from her little Harlem protégé, and definitely not in a classroom situation. A lecture ensued to correct my errors: Communism was the hope of the future, the faith of the poor. Stalin took a backward country and converted it into a military fortress capable of halting the Nazi onslaught. The Ribbentrop-Molotov pact of 1939 was tactical, not a shift in principles. It warded off an imperialist coalition that bought time for the Russians to arm.

No one else spoke, or dared to. So I hesitatingly brought up my sister's mixed experience in the Young Communist League: boyfriends virtually conscripted to enlist for the Lincoln Brigade to fight for the Spanish Republic—and some not coming home; the dominance of white membership in the Harlem YCL, while Negro backwardness was constantly bemoaned; the promised freedom by virtue of being a Communist, followed by endless didactics from the works of Lenin and Stalin; the unfailing committment to Soviet political lines on every single issue at the risk of being branded a deviationist.

I spoke with passion, if not with eloquence—the same sort of combative passion that marked my growing up. And it worked! The spirit of combat also existed in the intellectual realm. I felt the same exhilaration on winning, especially after class, when my new schoolmates whispered to me, "Nice going!" with pats on the back to boot. Overnight, or so it seemed at the time, I was transformed from class bully to class politician. The torturous YCL meetings I had to attend with my sister, alas paid off more handsomely for me than for her. For Paula, the terrible loss of her boyfriend, Milt Gordon, in the last days of the defense of Republican Madrid, followed by the Nazi-Soviet pact, led to her quiet retreat from politics—of which we never again spoke for the rest of her life.

It was sports, fortunately, that afforded me an outlet for my physical expression. How right William James was in his understanding of the sportive instinct as the displacement of warrior behavior by symbolic acts. As my mind became increasingly focused on the ordinary studies of an eighth-grader, my body gave itself over to the needs of playing football, baseball, and basketball. In each instance, the teachers were helpful. And in the world of sports, my less than civil behavior was a distinct advantage. It helped me score points, even if it also sometimes involved poor sportsmanship.

In short, the process of leaving Harlem was just that—a process, not simply an event. In Brooklyn, the atmosphere was less hostile but strangely more competitive. Mr. Gewirtz, the bespectacled principal, running his school like a training academy for college; "Doc" Whitman, whose efforts to reconstruct past history as living present thrilled us all; Mrs. Mims, the confirmed Communist, who nonetheless could teach grammar and rhetoric with the patience of a Christian saint—all confirmed a world to win beyond the physical: a triumph not of will, but of mind; of giving scope to imagination and liberating children from the terrible scourges of life and death, focusing our innocent attentions on the wonderful things in between.

So, in about the space of a school term, I became "socialized," not as in *A Clockwork Orange,* a brainwashed scourge on the body politic, but as a youngster permitted to participate in a world in which the Neo-Darwinian verities did not apply every waking day and sleepless night. And in this gradual way, I left Harlem in spirit as in body.

CHAPTER FOURTEEN

A man sets himself the task of making a plan of the
universe. After many years, he fills a whole space with
images of provinces, kingdoms, mountains, bays, ships,
islands, fish, rooms, instruments, stars, horses, and people.
On the threshold of death, he discovers that the patient
labyrinth of lines has traced the likeness of his own face.
Jorge Luis Borges, *El Hacedor*

Denouement

It would be facile but false to say that my interest in sociology
derived from my early days in Harlem. True, Harlem was a
sociological laboratory—a place one would expect good researchers to stem from. The social structure of the New York City
academic institutions, however, especially those in Manhattan,
inhibited the development of just such good researchers. For
years, Columbia University viewed Morningside Heights as a
barrier rather than as an opportunity. New York University was
weak in sociology; in any event, it was more concerned with social
drama and social-psychological role-playing than with the study
of social systems and stratification. City College was essentially an
undergraduate institution, and for years was relatively weak in
social-research areas other than history and philosophy.

In New York, the university was in permanent exile from the
community. It was driven by notions of civilization and powered
by its European discontents. Even institutions such as The New
School for Social Research were places largely inhabited by European exiles from reaction and national socialism. This, in contrast
to Chicago, for example, where the university was an integral part

of the community. The emphases were on urban growth versus urban blight, the life cycle of people and cultures, race relations, and mass education.

This may sound like a diversion. But, in fact, for a poor boy growing up in Harlem with an eye toward a university education, such structural factors loomed large. School administrators and professors alike discounted any belief in the importance of ghetto life in Harlem as a fit subject for higher learning.

School was an escape from reality, not its confirmation. Thirsting after book knowledge was not to reach a higher appreciation of local social conditions, but to give some sense of order to a larger universe, far removed, it was hoped, from the ordinary cares of the ghetto. From Tom Swift stories to stamp collecting, through which I learned a lot about exotic places and people, I strove to take flight from the ghetto—if not in daily life, then in the private life of my mind.

The most serious indication of this escapist mode was my decision to major in philosophy at City College. The very announcement of this at home brought forth groans and moans: "Not practical," my parents said, "a rich man's subject." My father thought of philosophy as "fool's gold"; something that could only lead to "eternal starvation." Being at least vaguely Jewish, at least he didn't invoke the phrase "eternal damnation." But what, in truth, was a young person from the streets of Harlem, separated from the blacks on one side and segregated from the whites on the other, to do? Philosophy was assuredly the secular side of rabbinical studies. And having grown up in a home largely devoid of religious instruction or sacral values, philosophy became a way to satisfy my longing for the eternal.

It wasn't, I should add, that I had no concern for the condition of the blacks in Harlem; rather, I raised it to a level of abstract concern for the working class in general. I turned my attention to ideological questions of the national status of minorities in America. Indeed, in the special program of City College, in which philosophy students were intimately involved in a social science honors program, social researchers from Marshall and Keynes in economics, to Toynbee and Spengler in history, to Durkheim and Weber in sociology, were all known to me. But, then, they were known as they were rendered—as abstractions. Part of a great men/ great books effort.

The pure, theoretical nature of the learning process lifted me out of the realm of ordinary life. I came to thirst after such abstractions. My idols were people like Morris Raphael Cohen, the Jewish Aristotle of City College, who became a heroic figure. There we were, in the bowels of Harlem, discoursing on critical realism, dialectical materialism, phenomenological analysis. My first essay was a critique of Plato and the closed society. My burning animus against Plato's fixed categories doubtless derived from growing up in Harlem. But that phase of my training was separated from empirical life. Even Marxism and socialism were dreamy ideologies that helped lift my spirits from grimy reality to glorious utopia.

Sociology took on meaning much later in my life: with the withering away of philosophy through the scalpel and the sword of the logical positivists. Like others of my generation, I was left with a method but no field of application; an ontological faith without any corresponding world view. The transition from philosophy to sociology was a long, painful, and essentially auto-didactic one. It involved a trip to South America and an immersion into the sociology of knowledge. It was through the study of the social conditions of ideas that I was in a position to examine the sociology of institutions. This trek took years. It was a spiritual journey as well as a cultural one.

Clearly, some residue, some concerns from my Harlem days, stuck fast and hard. But those days were followed by a long period of escape, anchored in the university of learning. It was only much later, when the chimeric nature of that escape became evident, that I was able to reflect with any frankness and honesty at all on those early days of pre-adolescence.

A tough life does not always yield rich insights and healthy social attitudes. In my case, every waking hour was dedicated to the art of survival and the goal of escape. Whatever "love of learning" I gained was only because music, literature, and the theater liberated me from the cares of the day. My revulsion for tendentiousness in art derives from the simple realization that everyday life has enough woes without importing them into cultural life.

It is only now, or in the relatively recent past, that a certain serenity has come to my life: in which a balance of sorts has been struck between the abstract and the concrete, the residues of poverty and the responsibilities of civility, making possible these intensely introspective reflections. There was no smooth transition from personal terrors to sociological thunderings. Becoming a sociologist was no simple matter. It came almost as hard and surely as reluctantly as growing up absurd in the streets of Black Harlem.

CHAPTER FIFTEEN

Life is full of contradictions. And the absolute is something very dangerous. Death is absolute; but otherwise for me, everything exists only in relation to something else. But I have no sense of absolute. It's always a relation I'm trying to understand—between people, between things. It is a scientific attitude and I respect it very much in the scientist. There is a truth at a certain moment, which is going to be questioned very quickly by another scientist, which is a real attitude, but not an eternal, permanent truth. Everything exists in relation.

Henri Cartier-Bresson (July 1975)

Picture-Taking Days

Photographs from my childhood years in Harlem are sparse. I realize now that picture-taking days were special; they usually occurred in conjunction with Sunday trips rather than with routine events. We had an old Brownie camera, the Kodak equivalent of the Ford Model-T, but we rarely had enough money for film to put in it.

The other problem is that so many pictures were lost along the way. Growing up poor does not equip one for immortality! Photographs were rarely duplicated, and negatives frequently misplaced. Still, there are enough existing pictures to give some idea of life in the Horowitz family.

For every one image of my own childhood days, I must have at least one hundred of those of my own two children. At this point in American time, "photo opportunities" are built into the routine of masses and elites alike. But that was scarcely the case in the pre-war period of 1929-1941. For example, these photographs of my mother, father, sister, and some other important relatives, as well as a few precious pictures of everyday life, are images that powerfully evoke for me a childhood long past.

My father (seated) on leave in Russia from the Austrian front in 1917 (seen with a younger brother, Jack) just before he sustained shrapnel wounds in both legs.

My parents and sister in 1920, just after my sister Paula's birth. Note that my sister literally sits on a pedestal!

My mother (top right corner) with two of her sisters (Jennie and Nessie) and one of my father's brothers, Asher. This picture was taken soon after my father left to go to the United States.

My mother and sister with the aunts and uncles in the Tepper line. This was taken in 1926, about two years before their departure to join my father in America. From left to right are Paula, Ruth, Motyl, Esther, and Sarah. The last figure on the right I cannot identify. I remember my mother saying that they all remained in the Soviet Union.

A reproduction of my father's Certificate of Naturalization, one of his most treasured possessions. My sister Paula is mistakenly called "Bessie" (the middle daughter in the Schneider family), and my father is listed as a citizen of "Poland-Russia"—a description that probably reflected his ambiguous feelings about national identity; or maybe just plain ambiguous borders at the time.

A Harlem street scene circa 1935. Part of the great Work Projects Administration series, this photograph records a typical summer day and could well have been taken on my own block; certainly in my immediate neighborhood.

The interior of my father's shop at 2270 Eighth Avenue. This is perhaps the most precious photograph I own. The table to the left at which my father cut glass, installed frames, and made window shades, frequently doubled as my bed. Through the portal directly behind my father was the kitchen. This was where our family lived and worked.

With my mother and father in Central Park. I am two years old.

My sister Paula at seventeen, when she graduated from Wadleigh High School in 1937. This picture, taken when she was still a beautiful young girl, is the way I shall always remember her.

My uncle Moses (Moises) and his wife Rachel. The only one of my father's brothers to emigrate from Russia, Moses went to Argentina where he became tailor to the National Assembly.

The two children of Moses Horowitz: Leonore and Isadore, as seen in 1938. Leonore went on to become a social worker. Isadore is now a well-known Argentine medical researcher.

My aunt and favorite relative, Jennie Schneider. The picture dates from the mid-1930s. She lived on until her mid-90s and was lucid and clever every step of the way.

My uncle Isadore (Izzy) Schneider, a pants cutter, flanked by his younger brothers Philip (to the left) and Jack (to the right). The Schneiders, who had settled in America long before my father and mother arrived, provided an important counterpoint to life at the Horowitz's.

Two of my father's brothers who remained in the Soviet Union. Joseph (left) became brigadier general during World War II. Nathan (right)—the only brother to leave the European for the Asian part of the country—became a forest ranger in the Ural Mountain region. This photo dates from 1919, and the woman in the photo is Jennie.

My parents and I, probably on a spring Sunday outing to Bensonhurst, Brooklyn, where the Schneiders lived. The house to the rear of us was certainly like nothing I recollect in Harlem.

A school picture taken in January 1944, the year after we left Harlem and settled in Brooklyn. I am standing third row from the top, third from the left. While I recollect these boys and girls vividly, alas, I have kept track of none of them. The names on the back of the photograph make me realize that this school had just about as many Irish and Italian youngsters as Jewish pupils. In retrospect, only the Protestants seem missing!